FAVOR

*F*AVOR

GOD'S GRACE
TO A MOTHER'S PRAYERS

WHAT MEN PRONOUNCED DEAD,
GOD MADE ALIVE

Lois Diane Pruitt

To order additional copies of this book, contact:
Xlibris Corporation
1-888-795-4274
www.Xlibris.com
Orders@Xlibris.com
89573

Contents

Dedication

I want to dedicate this book in memory of my grandparents, Rachel and Henry Pruitt and Luella and Johnnie Minor, who will forever live in my heart.

And also to the many families who have experienced the same situation such as I have. I have read about comatose patients, and I am so saddened by the fact that most doctors will encourage the family members to unplug their loved ones so soon. I encourage you to pray and be led by the Lord.

Illustrations

The first picture was LaRicko in the intensive care unit
Second picture was LaRicko moved to the pulmonary floor
Third picture was LaRicko first day at the rehabilitation intensive care unit
Fourth picture was LaRicko moved out of the intensive care unit
Fifth Picture was my Mother and Horace visiting LaRicko at the rehabilitation center
Sixth picture was LaRicko headed out to the movies
Seventh picture was LaRicko and Dad watching the fish in the pond
Eighth picture was LaRicko and Mom enjoying the beautiful outdoors at the facility
Ninth picture was LaRicko's surprise visit from his Aunt Doris and Uncle Bill
Tenth picture was the spoons that were specially made for LaRicko
Eleventh picture was LaRicko's first steps outside with his dad
Twelfth picture was LaRicko's first weekend walking outside with us
Thirteenth picture was LaRicko's visit to Arkansas for Thanksgiving, carving the turkey!
Fourteenth picture was LaRicko hanging the curtains that I saved faithfully for him
Fifteenth picture was LaRicko enjoying on a cruise ship
Sixteenth picture was LaRicko happy at home in Memphis!

Preface

The purpose of this book is to inspire and encourage families to always say a prayer (ASAP) and to lean not to our own understanding, but in all your ways acknowledge the Lord, and he will direct your path.

Acknowledgments

I'd like to thank my parents, Horace and Mable Pruitt, for always encouraging and supporting me. And most of all, I thank them for believing in me.

I want to thank my three brothers, Walter (Bud), Darrie (Daryl), and Horace (Baba) who have always been there for me!

Thank you to

Theresa Sanders, my best friend

Elder K. Allen
Minister S. Mullins

Special thanks to Byron for all the support you gave us.

Thanks to my Church family and my Pastor for all your prayers.

Thanks to all the Church families, friends, family members, and everyone who prayed for us through our crisis.

We love all of you!

Introduction

I have always prayed to recognize the Lord's voice when he is speaking to me, as well as to know when to follow the Holy Spirit. And as I went through the medical crisis with my son, I have been able to recognize the presence of the Lord more. I am yet a work in progress, but I have grown closer to that knowledge. I'd like to share with my audience some of the experiences that I had to go through in order for the Lord to prepare me for where I have come in my spiritual walk with him. After researching many books and surfing the Internet on comatose patients, I have discovered the recovery rate is significantly low. Even the doctors I encountered in the hospital tried to encourage me to unplug and let go of my son.

My story is to encourage families that are currently suffering with their loved ones who are in a comatose state. I know that this is one of the greatest battles in the medical field, but before just giving up or believing everything the doctors or specialists recommend, remember first to always say a prayer (ASAP). Ask the Lord what you want to know, be specific, and wait for your answer. Don't react in haste; take your time so you can make a decision that you are comfortable with.

In my walk with the Lord, I've learned to wait on all things for the right direction. As it is written in Galatians 5: 5, KJV, "For we through the Spirit wait for the hope of righteousness by faith." Your outcome may not be the same as mine, but I want to encourage you to always ask questions . . . never assume.

And with this in mind, I'd like to share my testimony. Just know that you cannot have the testimony without the test.

"My Walk through the Valley Journal"

On Saturday, July 26, 2003, *my son LaRicko and his fiancée who was residing in Memphis, Tennessee, came home to St. Louis for the weekend. I'll never forget how excited I was the whole week, knowing they were coming. But at the same time, my week seemed rather unusual. I was rushing around trying to get so many things done. I remember saying to myself, I hope nothing is going to happen. The feeling was so intense as well as strange.*

Well, after LaRicko got here to St. Louis, my best friend and I went over to his future in-laws' house to pick him up. We rode around a little bit in my best friend's new car, and then we came to my house where we sat around talking and laughing about old times as well as cooking and eating. The evening was great. We stayed up extremely late just enjoying each other's company.

*   **On Sunday, July 27,** *I got up early and prepared breakfast for LaRicko before leaving for church, but I didn't wake him up before I left because we'd stayed up so late the night before, and he was going to drive back to Memphis later on that day. So I let him rest.*

*   Well, I left and went to church, and for some reason, Sunday morning services felt unusual. I'll never forget the choir sang **"He will never put more on you than you can bear."** The whole time they were singing, tears kept running down my face. My pastor was out of town that Sunday, and one of the other ministers of the church preached, and as interesting as it may seem, his sermon felt as if it was just for me, because he preached from **Hebrews 11:1.**

*   **Now faith is the substance of things hoped for, the evidence of things not seen.**

*   **And his topic was unseen evidence**. *(God knows where to deliver your mail.)*

*   When I came home from church, I met LaRicko at the front of the house at the steps. He'd just come back home from visiting with a friend in the neighborhood. We gave each other a hug as we proceeded into the house. As I put my things away, we went into the kitchen and sat down at the table, and we continued to laugh and talk about so many things. We even talked about the rough times we'd shared together. When I'd lost my job, I reminded him how we used to repeat the twenty-third Psalm, and I'd always say, "As we walk through the*

valley" because we are not going to stay here; we'd always think the positive regarding the outcome. We got up and walked to the living room because I was in the process of changing the curtains, and I wanted his suggestion on the color. Well, he said I should change the curtains from navy blue to a cream color. And I took him up on his suggestion. So we headed back to the kitchen and sat down again, where we began to converse even more. After a while, I noticed he started to nod off to sleep, and I said to him, "You can't get on the road still sleepy, and he said, "Mom, once I get started driving on the road, I'll be okay."

We were also invited to his future in-laws' later in the afternoon for dinner, but since he was nodding, I suggested that he take a nap first. And while he was taking a nap, I decided to run out to the store and purchase some cream curtains so that he could see them prior to going back home to Memphis. When I got back home from shopping, I didn't disturb him because he was snoring so loud, so I assumed he was extremely tired. So instead, I went to his future in-laws for dinner without him and decided to just bring his dinner back with me so that he could eat it when he woke up. Three and a half hours later when I returned home, he was still snoring, so I decided to wake him to tell him to turn over and get comfortable so that he could stop snoring. At this point, I couldn't get him to wake up. I went to the bathroom, I got a towel, I wet it with cold water, and I placed it on his forehead; he did not flinch. I picked up the phone and called my mother, and she suggested that I call 911 right away.

When the emergency team showed up at my house, they began to check him over, not being able to find the problem. Then my son was given a shot, which was not the right thing to do because I heard them say, "He is starting to seize, let's get him to the hospital." I could not believe my world was crumbling right before my eyes.

When we got to the hospital, they took me, his dad, and his fiancée to this small area where we waited until the doctor, who was running test on LaRicko, returned with the diagnosis. The first time the doctor entered the room, he said that it appeared that my son had a stroke because his right side seem to have been paralyzed. I was speechless to see that LaRicko was so young and was just starting to live. Then the doctor included that they weren't sure; they were going to continue to check him out.

The doctor left the room for a while and came back and said he may have had an aneurysm. I was just so outdone at the diagnosis. Well, as if I hadn't heard enough, the doctor left again to do further testing and came back for the third time and said it looked as if he may have had meningitis. I just didn't know what to think at this point.

On Monday, July 28, *just when I thought I'd heard it all, the final diagnosis was he'd had a seizure in his sleep, and there was not enough oxygen flowing to the brain for more than three to four hours. I was told that the brain can only go without oxygen for up to four minutes; after that, the brain is dead, and there's no way that the brain can be repaired.*

They placed LaRicko in the intensive care unit and allowed us to go in and see him. As I looked at my son and how healthy he appeared, I began to pray and ask the Lord to heal him. I know that my God is a healer. Shortly after that, they informed me that they were calling a top specialist to give us the final diagnosis. This took about an hour.

We were all sitting in the waiting area when the specialist came out and sat at the table with us. He began to tell us that LaRicko was completely brain-dead and that there's absolutely nothing they could do about his situation. The neurologist said that they could jump-start hearts when they stop, but never a brain. He said LaRicko's brain was like an egg placed in a skillet; once the brain is fried, there's nothing else that they can do. He suggested that I unplug him because he'd never be anything but a vegetable. He described LaRicko as a car without a motor. The doctor then asked me, "Why would you want to keep a car without a motor?" The neurologist's closing words for that night were "I am the little god, you need to call on the big God," and he continue with "Let me know what day you want to unplug your son." I shook his hand and thanked him for his services. That's when I chose to call on the big God. I knew at this point, I had to reach for Dr. Jesus. Everyone around me started to cry. But I knew in my heart that no matter how many tears I shed that night, the tears could not bring LaRicko back. So I didn't waste any time crying. I began to pray and ask the Lord to order my steps because at this point, I didn't know what to do.

On Tuesday, July 29, *as I walked into the intensive care unit to visit with my son, there was a nurse standing there changing his IV tubes. I spoke to her and asked, "How is he doing today?" She said, "He is doing the same" as she continued to look in the opposite direction, never looking up at me. I asked, "So there haven't been any changes?" She stopped what she was doing, looked up at me with a look that I will never forget, and said, "Be realistic, there is no way he is going to make it out of here." I stood there, not believing anyone could be so inconsiderate and coldhearted. I said, "Okay, and thank you for watching over him." I sat at my son's bedside, and I began to pray and talk to him as if he was* *going to respond to me. I remember saying "I've always talked to you about faith, and I've explained to you that you only need faith the size of a mustard seed, which I know you have at least that much, so with that in mind, we're going to make it out of this."*

On Wednesday, July 30, *when I entered the intensive care unit to see my son, there was a different nurse. This particular nurse was very compassionate. She encouraged me to continue to pray because God is the one who is in control, no matter what the doctors are saying. I was so happy to hear that from this nurse, and I continued to pray. LaRicko's condition continued on through* **Thursday, Friday, and Saturday**; *he was still in a coma.*

On Sunday, August 3, *I was sitting in the intensive care waiting room when I received a call on my cell phone. The call was to inform me that LaRicko's brother and my grandson had been in a motorcycle accident, and they were in the emergency room down the hall. I started to pray and remember that the Lord said in his Word that he will never put more on me than I can bear.*

On Monday, August 4, *the doctor that was taking care of LaRicko decided to step down while another doctor took over. When she came to me that morning, she said, "We will give your son another week just to see if we can get some kind of response from him, but at the end of the week if there's not any responses, then we will know that LaRicko is completely brain-dead and there will never be any changes." This doctor, just as the other doctor, stated that once the brain is dead, there's absolutely nothing that can be done about this. The doctor also stated that if that is the case, then I will need to unplug LaRicko or release him* *to a nursing home because he couldn't continue his stay there at their hospital in that condition.*

On Tuesday, August 5, *the doctor came and spoke with me that morning, and I inquired about a second opinion. The doctor told me that she'd check on my request and get back to me. About a half an hour later, the floor nurse came out to speak with me, and she informed me that the doctor sent her out to let me know that if I chose to get a second opinion on my son, she'd no longer be his doctor. At that point, I had nowhere else to turn to but to Dr. Jesus. I prayed to God to order my steps because if I had to unplug my son, I would have also needed a sign from God to do so. Well, as that day went on, a nurse came to me and said a brain specialist just spoke with her and agreed to give me a second opinion on LaRicko.*

Later on that day after the doctor had completely examined LaRicko; the nurse came out and spoke with me and LaRicko's father. When we went back to LaRicko's room, the doctor began to tell us that LaRicko's brain was not completely dead, but it was severely damaged. I got excited, but the doctor insisted that I shouldn't build my hopes up because the brain was severely damaged. He still felt that there was not enough activity going on in the brain to get a positive diagnosis regarding his condition.

On Wednesday, August 6, *I was told that LaRicko's doctor would no longer be his physician, so I prayed for another physician for him. And later on that day, a friend of mine who worked for the hospital at that time came to me and said she had spoken with a doctor on her floor, and she explained to him the situation we were dealing with, and this doctor* said he would be glad to take LaRicko on as his patient. God just kept on showing up for us.

On Thursday, August 7, Friday, August 8; and Saturday, August 9, things appeared to be the same. I'd go into LaRicko's room, and I'd talk to him as if he's going to respond. I'd repeat the twenty-third psalm every time I entered my son's room, but LaRicko still did not respond.

On Sunday, August 10, as I entered LaRicko's room, I found a nurse checking his blood pressure. The nurse informed me that he was going to slowly take LaRicko off sedation, just to see how LaRicko would react. As he took my son off slowly, it appeared to me that LaRicko was trying to respond and also appeared to me that he was experiencing some type of pain. The doctor said that LaRicko couldn't possibly be reacting to any type of pain because his brain is dead. I tried to explain to the doctor that my son was responding to me, but the doctor told me that the body will flex if the brain is dead. So they ruled out what I thought were responses to be just reflexes from a brain-dead body.

On Monday, August 11, I complained so much about LaRicko appearing to be in pain that the doctor reluctantly ordered a pain patch to be placed on him just before they moved him out of the intensive care unit. LaRicko was placed on another floor so that the doctor who agreed to take him on as a patient could take over at that point. Later on that afternoon, LaRicko was really going through some rough times. His oxygen levels on the life-support machine had to be increased because he was not breathing on his own. LaRicko had seen better days.

On Tuesday, August 12, LaRicko's second day out of the intensive care unit was worse than the day before. His temperature had gone up *to 102, which was not good. There had been a change in his medication, so I felt that the medication was not agreeing with my son's system. I spoke with the nurse regarding LaRicko's condition, and she advised me that because my son is completely brain-dead, there's a splint in the brain that regulates the body temperature, and being that LaRicko is completely brain-dead, his splint is no longer functioning which is why his temperature will continue to elevate; this would remain until he dies. So as the day went on, his temperature continued to elevate.*

On Wednesday, August 13, as our day went on, I just watched my son get worse and worse. He'd flex and frown as if he was experiencing severe pain. The nurse would apply cold packs to LaRicko's head because of the elevation of the temperature, but the doctor said to me again that the body experience reflexes when the brain is dead and LaRicko had no way of knowing that he's in pain. I was told that all these reactions were just coming from LaRicko being brain-dead.

On Thursday, August 14, just when I thought we'd experienced enough bad issues, LaRicko started to get more and more irritated, but needless to say, no one saw things my way. The staff would continue to explain to me that this was a normal function for a dead brain. They continued with "LaRicko's body will continue to go through different stages because of that." Afterward, I'd continue to sit and watch my son's body go through all kinds of changes. Each moment that I watched LaRicko go through these changes, it got harder and harder for me.

On Friday, August 15, I stayed all day with LaRicko and watched his condition continue to worsen. He'd kick as if he was trying to fight his way out of something, and his temperature kept spiking up along with his blood pressure. The staff placed a cart for me to sleep on in his room. I spent the night with him to observe his continued restlessness. LaRicko didn't rest at all.

On Saturday, August 16, LaRicko's temperature was really out of control. The staff started placing more cold packs on my son just to try and cool his body down, but nothing was working. After hours of not being able to control the temperature, the doctor requested to have him placed on a bed of ice in order to try and cool LaRicko's body temperature down. That was another rough day that I watched my son's body go through unbelievable changes.

On Sunday, August 17, the medical technicians and the nurse had taken so much blood from LaRicko the night before in attempt to see what was going on with his body. After testing my son's blood over and over, the doctor said it appeared that LaRicko had blood clots in his legs. I was not at all convinced with those results. As that day went on, the nurses placed equipment on both of my son's legs in an attempt to circulate the blood in his legs. LaRicko's appearance was starting to change at this point.

On Monday, August 18, when the doctor noticed that LaRicko's blood pressure was not coming down, they placed him on blood pressure medication. And even after that, LaRicko's blood pressure continued to increase. All day long, the focus was on LaRicko's blood pressure and the blood clots that were in his legs.

On Tuesday, August 19, the doctors were finally convinced that they needed to call in another specialist to determine what was going on with LaRicko's temperature and blood pressure. They also kept seeing something going on in his blood. First they thought my son *had blood clots in his legs, but later the staff noticed that blood clots weren't the case. So the doctor brought in an infection specialist who took blood samples from LaRicko and ran several other tests on him most of the day.*

On Wednesday, August 20, *after running the test on my son, the infection specialist discovered that they were giving LaRicko an antibiotic that did not agree with his system. This antibiotic caused LaRicko's temperature to increase and caused his tongue and throat to break out with a rash called thrush. This was really bad because LaRicko also had a tracheotomy in his throat, which was causing that area of his neck to look really bad. LaRicko had a feeding tube in his stomach, IV in his arm, and a cathedra on him; as if things weren't bad enough, it seemed as if each day, his condition was getting worse.*

On Thursday, August 21, *I was standing in my son's room talking to him and praying with him as I always did. After a while, I sat down in a chair and started looking out of the window. It was raining very, very hard, and as I looked out, I began to pray to God. I'd quoted several scriptures from the Bible. After I finished my prayer, I looked over at my son, and he looked as if he was trying to sit up. I stood on my feet and rushed over to his bedside. I asked LaRicko, "If you want to sit up, blink once at me," and he did blink once for me. So I placed my arms behind his back, and a nurse walked into the room and began to assist me. While I helped my son to sit up in his bed, he moved his head as if he was looking to his left, then he moved as if he were looking to the right of the room. Suddenly LaRicko burst out with a laugh. We laid him back down, and I was so happy to feel my son was going to be okay. But it still remained. LaRicko's doctors and nurses said that he is brain-dead, and his body again is going through reflexes.*

On Friday, August 22, my son had another rough day. All day long, there was one issue after another. When I came into LaRicko's room, he was lying there looking as if he was down to his last breath. I saw that his IV was out of his arm and blood was all over his gown. I didn't know how long LaRicko had been lying up like this, so I immediately called for a nurse to come and take care of this issue. It was as though nobody cared because my son was brain-dead, and the staff seemed to just be waiting on him to stop breathing. The nurse finally came in and placed the IV in my son's arm again. Later on that evening, we notice LaRicko's arm getting extremely huge. We came to find out the medication was just running in his arm; the IV was not placed correctly in his vein. Go figure! We were in for another sleepless night because my son's breathing was really bad; his ventilator had to be turned on a higher level.

On Saturday, August 23, was the actual day that he and his fiancée were to become husband and wife, and he was still lying in the hospital in a coma, not even realizing that he was still in this world. As the day went on, I noticed that LaRicko's face started to twitch. Here again, things just kept on changing. The nurse came in later that evening to change the tubes on the ventilator; she had so many problems with doing this task. It went from one extreme to another. She broke a piece of the ventilator off and had to call backup because my son needed the oxygen from the ventilator to breath in order to stay alive. This was another horrible day!

On Sunday, August 24, after another rough night, believe it or not, the doctor ordered that my son's ventilator tube to be cleaned. I was really concerned about this because of yesterday's issues. Well, guess what, after the nurses finish the cleaning of LaRicko's ventilator, the tube kept popping off the machine. Each time this occurred, this caused

LaRicko to be without oxygen. I was concerned about this because my son's brain had already lost enough oxygen.

On Monday, August 25, we had a hard time just trying to keep my son comfortable. LaRicko took medication to try and calm him down, but nothing ever worked. I'd rub my son's hands and talk to him to let him know I was there and to try and calm down. This went on all day!

On Tuesday, August 26, once again we were headed for another rough day after no rest through the night. LaRicko appeared to be afraid to go to sleep; he'd just continue to twitch and kick his legs uncontrollably. His body was doing all kinds of strange movements. That went on for quite some time. During all these other issues, LaRicko was not having a bowel movement. That was another concern, along with the irritations around his neck and stomach. That was a sad situation!

On Wednesday, August 27, with all the craziness that was going on with LaRicko, the doctor approached me with the question regarding what I was going to do with my son. The caseworker insisted that I take him home with me or place him in a nursing home until he expired because he would never be anything but a vegetable. The doctor included at this point that my son was completely brain-dead because by now if he wasn't, he'd be showing different signs with the body, but LaRicko's body was only showing reflexes as a dead body would. She assured me that. At that point of his illness, there would be absolutely no changes in my son's condition. The caseworker said that LaRicko needed to be moved from their facility because there was nothing else that the doctors could do for him. As I said before, things kept getting worse for us. I asked the doctor if we could place him in a rehabilitation center because I felt the need for rehabilitation, but the doctor said to *me, "LaRicko would only be accepted by a nursing home facility here in the state." The doctor also stated that a rehabilitation facility would never take my son because of the tube in his throat, the feeding tube in his stomach, the ventilator, and the I.V. in his arm. Then I was told that the only rehabilitation facility that would accept my son was four hours away from home. Wow!*

On Thursday, August 28, after a very disturbing day yesterday learning that I must make a decision to have LaRicko removed from the facility because the doctors had done all that they could do for him, I was pressured. When I entered my son's room on this date, I went to lean over to kiss him as usual; I noticed his right arm was swollen about three sizes larger than the norm. I pressed the call button to contact a nurse. When the nurse walked in, she said to me again that his IV was not placed in his arm correctly and they didn't realize it until my son's arm had blown up like a balloon. I was really being tested with my faith. I felt that my son knew if anybody would fight to keep him alive that it would be his mother. I can't give up now!

On Friday, August 29, of course it was another day of wondering what was going to happen next. LaRicko was just lying there looking straight ahead; I kept waving my hands in front of his eyes praying that my son would eventually blink and show me some sign of improvement so that we could get out of this hospital which couldn't wait to get rid of us, but LaRicko couldn't see me. Nothing had changed . . . My son was in a deep coma. I spoke with the caseworker of the hospital to let her know the decision I made. I decided to let LaRicko go to the rehabilitation facility that was four hours away. After another long day, I stayed the night with my son once again. Through the night, the nurse would come in very quietly and say to me, "You need to talk to

him, tell him he is in the hospital, and explain to him why he is here."
Well, I was on one side of the bed, and she was on the other; when she
said to tell him he was in the hospital, LaRicko started to frown up as
he began to cry. I got a little upset with the nurse because she appeared
to be upsetting my son. That was the first time I'd seen that nurse,
so I had questioned another nurse about her. The other nurse had
informed me that this particular nurse was a very religious woman.
I was pleased with that, but I still didn't appreciate her upsetting my
son. So each time she'd come in, I'd watch her very closely while she
would check my son's blood pressure and temperature. And of all the
times, I noticed that it appeared that LaRicko was actually watching
her as well. I thought that was a bit strange being that he never
responded to any of the other nurses; there was something different
about that nurse. I just didn't want her to say anything else about my
son being in the hospital in front of him because I knew how much
LaRicko feared hospitals.

On Saturday, August 30, I needed to focus on the decision that I
made on what I was going to do with my son. I was already informed
that the facilities here in the city limits would not accept LaRicko, and
the only facility that would was four hours away. I knew at this point
that I needed to go and visit that facility. So my best friend called and
said to me, "I think it's time for us to take a drive and check this place
out." I went to the hospital and checked on my son before I left and
went to see the rehabilitation center, and he appeared to be stable today.
LaRicko's Aunt Lela sat with him while we made the trip.

On Sunday, August 31, my son was still pretty stable at that
point. We're concerned about LaRicko because he had not had bowel
movement. We couldn't understand what was going on with my son's

body. The whole day was just a period of praying and waiting on God to answer prayers.

On Monday, September 1, *as we headed into another day, one positive thing happened for us which was LaRicko finally had a bowel movement. This was really a concern to the nurses and the doctor as well as me, and we were very happy about that. Thank God for a bowel movement!*

On Tuesday, September 2, *it was another waiting game to see if any changes were going to occur. The nurses during the day really appeared to have dropped the ball; they didn't seem to be taking care of LaRicko like I felt they should. That afternoon, the caseworker informed me that my son was denied by the facility that I prayed long and hard about. She said they wouldn't take him because he was in a coma with tubes in his throat and stomach. They couldn't accept a patient in that condition. Well, now I didn't know what to do except continue to pray and ask the Lord for a facility that is best for LaRicko. When the nurse came in on the second shift after being off for several days, he was very disappointed to see that my son had not been taken cared of like he should have been. He was concerned about the unusual discoloration on LaRicko's throat area, which hadn't been taken care of like it should have been. That area on my son's neck had become infected. The nurse began to clean LaRicko up and really took care for him that day. LaRicko appeared to look and feel much better afterward. So my son rested much better throughout that night.*

On Wednesday, September 3, *this was another day that we were back to square one on the unconcerned staff. The staff really had begun to take my son's condition lightly. My son was not showing any signs* of improvement. At this point, the whole staff realized that they had a brain-dead patient lying here, and LaRicko would never be or do anything more at this point but expire. I was really concerned by the lack of care there. LaRicko's bowel movements had stopped again, and he appeared to be miserable all over again.

On Thursday September 4, it was another day of trying to really grasp why no one really felt what I was feeling. No one could believe that I actually felt that my son was going to be okay if he could go to a rehabilitation facility. LaRicko's blood pressure and temperature was still higher than it should have been. My son would frown often as if he were in pain, and that had been going on for days, but we were being told as usual that there was no way he could have known that he was in pain because LaRicko had no brain activity going on for him to recognize pain. LaRicko had lost so much weight, and his hands had retracted under. He really was looking bad. The caseworker at the hospital spoke with me regarding packing LaRicko's things and taking him home.

On Friday, September 5, this was another day praying for my son to have a bowel movement. We needed something positive to happen at this point. It's been rough. On the second shift when the nurse and the second-shift tech came into my son's room, I said, "Thank God they were back." The nurse was saddened again over my son's condition. The nurse and the tech knew that my son was not being taken care of like he should have been. I was always happy for that nurse and that medical tech to come in on Fridays. They would at least clean LaRicko up. My mother came from Arkansas, and my youngest brother came from Memphis to visit me and LaRicko for that weekend. Mom and Horace saw that my son wasn't appearing to get any better, and they noticed that *his face showed that he was experiencing some type of pain somewhere in his body. LaRicko's body was just deteriorating as days went on.*

On Saturday, September 6 *my brother had spent the night with my son to give me and LaRicko's fiancée a break because we had spent so much time at the hospital. This was another day that he was expressing lots of pain in his left arm; he'd draw up his body and his left arm and frown really bad. I finally convinced the weekend doctor that he was having pain, so the doctor ordered some muscle relaxers for LaRicko to take to see if that would help him. We prayed that my son would at least feel better from the medication. My mother and I sat with him all day. She monitored LaRicko as well. Later that day, he did eventually have a bowel movement. Thank God for the small miracles!*

On Sunday, September 7, *my mother and my youngest brother visited with me and LaRicko most of the day until they left to head back home. This was another day that LaRicko was just lying there. My son showed no expressions; he just appeared to have been going down really bad. So I stood at his bedside talking to him and praying with him.*

On Monday, September 8, *I went to the hospital, entered LaRicko's room, and discovered his tube in his throat had detached from the ventilator. When I spoke to the nurse, she said she hadn't been in his room for about twenty minutes and no one else had checked on my son. I thank God that he was there for LaRicko, because some of the nurses didn't show that they cared at all.*

On Tuesday, September 9, *I'll never forget when I walked into my son's room that afternoon and looked at his legs. The leg massages had been removed from his legs, and he obviously had been kicking because* his legs had gotten caught in the bed rails. His legs were all scarred up, and he'd already had a sore on the back of his left ear. I was really disturbed at this point because when a patient starts breaking down with bedsores, it's really not a good thing; it's not easy, if ever, to get those wounds to heal. When I questioned the nurse regarding what happened to the massagers on my son's legs, she didn't know who took them off or why they took them off LaRicko's legs. The nurse did not know why no one was watching him either. But of course, no one knew what or how that incident happened. More and more each day, I could see that they knew there was no help for my son. The staff was done with trying to care for him. I just stood there looking at how my son's hands were bent under at the wrist and how he had lost so much weight. I didn't want him to suffer much longer. I prayed for a sign from the Lord to make it plain to me whether I should unplug LaRicko or not.

On Wednesday, September 10, *I was still a bit sad from the day before's issues, but I had to realize that no one really cared about my son like me. I felt that I needed to hold on to him a while longer. I knew my God can change all that. As that day went on and I looked at my son looking almost lifeless, I trusted that God was going to work this out for us.*

On Thursday, September 11, *once again I walked into my son's room to discover that his IV was out of his arm again, blood was all over his gown, and he was lying there looking even worse. You would have thought that I would have just given up. Each day it was proven that it was time to leave that hospital with my son; they moved LaRicko from his room that he'd been in for over forty days to another room. I knew it was time to go. The caseworker called me and told me the rehabilitation facility that had denied my son earlier called and agreed to accept him. She was really surprised and happy for me that the facility* had changed their decision and allowed my son the opportunity to come to the facility for rehab treatments. Prayer changes things. **God showed up and showed out!**

On Friday, September 12, *while I was sitting there with my son, his doctor came in and preformed a C-PAP on LaRicko; this is a procedure that allows us to know if his breathing is getting any better. The doctor had begun to talk to me regarding LaRicko's condition. He was such a nice doctor who kept my son at the hospital until I made a decision on where I was going to take my son.*

On Saturday, September 13, *LaRicko's dad and I were there visiting with LaRicko when LaRicko looked as if he wanted to sit up once again. His dad got on one side of him while I was on the other; we placed our hands behind his back very carefully and sat him up. As we held him up in a sitting position, LaRicko said,* **"This feel so good."** *His dad and I were so excited. Those were the first words we'd heard from LaRicko in over forty days. I began to thank God for baby steps!*

On Sunday, September 14, *while visiting with my son and praying as always, I was talking to him and combing his hair, and LaRicko asked me—yes, I said my son asked me—* **"Mom, what's wrong with me?"** *I was so excited. No one else was around to hear this, so when I told the doctor and the nurse what had happened, they said there was no way he could be talking to me with a tube down his throat. But I kept praying for God to show them because they really didn't believe me.*

On Monday, September 15, *after my son actually spoke to me on that Sunday, I stood by his bedside talking to him, explaining to him that we'd gone as far as we could go at that hospital, and a rehabilitation* center had accepted him to come there. I also explained to him how far away it was, and I asked him what he thought about this idea. He responded by looking as if he wanted to cry, but I asked him if he wanted to get better. I told LaRicko to blink for me if he wanted to get better. I explained to my son that the rehabilitation center is the best placed for him to recover and that I prayed and asked the Lord for rehab and not a nursing home for him. It was hard for me as well, but this was the best for my son.

On Tuesday, September 16, I was at work when I received a call from the hospital regarding taking LaRicko to surgery. This really caught me off guard. I rushed to the hospital, and when I got there, they were prepping him for this process. This procedure was going to be better for my son because he'd been stuck in his arms like a pin cushion for days, and the IV kept coming out of his arms; the doctors wanted to do this process prior to LaRicko being transferred to the next facility. The rest of the day, my son was very still.

On Wednesday, September 17, we had one more day there at the hospital, and my son hadn't spoken to me since that Sunday. Of course, the staff at that point thought this situation had caused me to actually lose my mind because I was constantly told that LaRicko couldn't possibly be able to speak with a tube in his throat. LaRicko's brain was dead with no activity there at all, so the doctors said. I can't convince them at all that my son spoke to me or that he was responding to me by blinking. I continued to pray and trust God to work this out for me. Show the staff that you are a miracle-working God!

On Thursday, September 18, that was the morning that we were leaving the hospital. While the staff was preparing LaRicko to leave

Lois Diane Pruitt

their facility, I prayed that this is the right thing for us to do since my son was going to be taken four hours away from home. The doctor entered LaRicko's room. She stood on one side of my son's bed while I stood on the other, and she looked at LaRicko, looked at me, and she said, "My final say is, your son is completely brain-dead, and there will be absolutely no changes in him." The doctor included that maybe in two to three years, my son may be able to be winged off the ventilator, but he will always remain a vegetable for the rest of his life. The doctor also included she was sorry. So I thanked her for everything that she'd done for us, and we proceeded to leave the hospital.

On Friday, September 19, it was our actual first full day at the rehabilitation facility; LaRicko appeared to be more alert. Not that he was out of the coma, but he had started talking. The doctor that was caring for my son came in at 9:21 a.m. and spoke with us to let us know his thoughts about LaRicko and to let us know the processes that the staff were going to be taking.

On Saturday, September 20, that was another interesting day. The doctor that was going to be caring for my son, who had never come in to work on a weekend before, actually came in just to see LaRicko. He had his staff came in with him. When the staff entered the room with the doctor, he ordered them to turn off the ventilator and remove the tube from my son's throat and place a mouthpiece over the area in LaRicko's throat. The doctor had this process done so that LaRicko could speak through it. LaRicko was in a coma, yet he was talking.

Chapter 1

My Life Turned Upside Down in One Day!

Just when I thought I had *experienced the raising of my son—from the changing of his diapers, sleepless nights when he didn't feel good, to teaching him how to walk and go potty, through teaching him how to say cute little words such as mommy, enjoying watching him grow up, nursing the skinned knees, wiping the tears from his eyes after bumps and bruises, to going to his competitive games rooting him on! As I watched him grow into the wonderful young man that he was, I prayed for the day that he'd say to me, "Mom, I'm getting married" so that I could also look forward to the loving grandbabies.*

Well, as time went on, he decided to move to another state to inaugurate a career there, which he felt was a great idea. And in such a short time, LaRicko and his fiancée had launched very good careers. Not only that, they both were really enjoying the area that they were residing in at the time too. I was so excited because it appeared that my son was growing up to be a young man who was getting life in the right perspective. Shortly after that, he and his fiancée had spoken to me about them having an October wedding. I was so happy and felt that my prayers were finally being answered.

One morning as I was lying in bed before getting dressed for work, a strange feeling came over me that I was going to be getting a grandbaby real soon. Hmm . . . I thought to myself. What was that? But needless to say, I was so excited over the thought as well, but I knew that my son would have shared the news with me if that was the case. So after I got to work that day, as the day went on, I picked up the phone and called my son's fiancée and asked her if she had something to tell me, and she chuckled and said, "Like what?" I asked her, "Well, am I going to be a grandmother soon?" And she chuckled again and said no! She asked, "What made you think something of that sort?" And I explained to her that it was just a feeling I had early that morning, so I just thought I'd ask. As the conversation went on, my son's fiancée and I chuckled about it and moved on to discussing other things. Well, as a couple more days passed and I still had the exciting feeling of becoming a grandmother, when I spoke with my son and his fiancée once again regarding that subject, they began to think I was starting to be comical, so his fiancée said to me, "We'll go to the doctor next week so that we can prove to you that the grandbaby feeling was not true." So we chuckled as we hung up the phone.

Well, as the time went on, there it was the next week, and they went to the doctor. I'll never forget the call I received at work in the month of

July. Guess what! She was pregnant, and I was actually going to become a grandmother. I was thinking to myself, Wow! My son was going to be a father, and each step in his life was getting ready to mature to another level. I finally felt that I was not responsible for taking care of my son anymore because he was taking on his own responsibilities. Awesome! That was a great feeling!

Things were getting even more exciting for me when my son and his fiancée called and said, "Our plans have changed for the wedding date." They decided to change the date to August 23 instead of October, which sounded very good to me. So as you can see, I was enjoying all that.

In the last week of July, I had a pretty unusual feeling all week long. I felt so rushed about everything, not understanding it. But I've always prayed for clear understanding, but I just couldn't grasp that one. My son had called and told me that he and his fiancée were coming up to visit over the weekend, and of course, you knew how excited I was about that.

On Saturday when they were to come up, my son had worked extremely long hours the night before, getting off from work early that morning and getting right on the road to come up here to St. Louis. I'll never forget when I spoke with my son on the phone; he appeared to be upset about coming to St. Louis. I couldn't understand that, other than he must have been very tired. So I asked LaRicko what was the problem, and he said, "I just don't like St. Louis, and I don't want to come up there." But he and his fiancée were bringing his fiancée's sister back here where she resides, and it was just for a day or so. But all of a sudden, LaRicko was not happy about the trip. There again, I just prayed and continued to run errands and take care of things here

*so that when they made it here, I could free myself up to spend quality
time with the both of them.*

*Later that day, I called LaRicko's dad to ask him if he'd install two
ceiling fans for me. Of course, his dad wanted to wait 'til the following
week, and I'll never forget how that really upset me. "No! I want them
done today," I said. I really felt I needed things done now as if I was
running out of time. So Chester did come over and installed the ceiling
fans for me that day, and he asked me what was the big rush. I explained,
"I don't know, I just felt that something was going to happen, but I don't
know what." I was praying that it was going to be all good things, but
God knows what's best for us even when we don't realize it.*

*LaRicko had made it later that afternoon. He and his fiancée stopped
by my house briefly and went to his future in-laws to visit with them
afterward. My best friend and I went out shopping and just hung out for
a while during the early part of the evening. That night while we were
out, I decided to call my son to see what they were doing. He said he'd
lain down for a while and fell asleep, and now he was just watching TV,
so I told him that we would be over to pick him up.*

*After picking LaRicko up, we drove around for a little while in my
best friend's new car. LaRicko was really admiring how nice Theresa's
new red Santa Fe was. And when we got back to my house, Theresa,
LaRicko, and I sat around the kitchen, laughing and talking about old
times. We were cooking and eating, just enjoying the night. We stayed up
'til around 1:00 a.m. or so.*

*The next morning, I got up and prepared breakfast for my son so that
when he got out of bed, the food would already be there for him being*

*that I was leaving for church. And once I got to church, I sat down to enjoy the service, and all of a sudden, I felt so sentimental. Especially when the choir began to sing the song with these lyrics, "He will never put more on you than you can bear!" I cried through the whole song, not understanding why that song would have touched me to that extent at the time. I love the song, but for some reason, it came across me that day in a very different way. That Sunday morning my pastor was out of town, and another minister preached. The minister's sermon that morning was from the book of **1 Kings 6:8-12** and also from **Hebrews 11:1,** and of course, we know that this book is talking about now faith! And the minister's sermon subject was on **Unseen Evidence**. And through that whole sermon, again I felt that it was all being preached for me for some reason. I kept that program from that Sunday morning, and I noticed on the program where I jotted down something that the minister had said through his preaching, which was "**believe in angels because you're God's special child, and you'll never be alone.**" You never know why things are placed in your spirit until you actually need it!*

After I returned home from church that afternoon, I was walking up the driveway when I saw my son walking up toward the house as well. We both met at the steps of the house, and he gave me a hug, and we went in together. He told me that he had just come back from visiting with a friend around the corner. I said to him, "You have to be careful of the people that you consider a friend." And LaRicko said to me, "Oh, Mom, George is cool." And I reminded him that everyone is not always happy to hear of another person's success. "Be careful of who you share your business with," I said. In the meantime, we both continued enjoying talking about things that used to go on with us and the different things that went on around the neighborhood. While LaRicko and I were continuing to spend the quality time that we had left together before *he and his fiancée were going to get on the road later that evening to head back to Memphis, I shared with LaRicko how happy I was for him and his fiancée. He was excited as well. And in the process, I began to show LaRicko different things that I had done around the house since he had been gone. As we walked through the house, I pointed out the new blinds I'd placed in the living room and dining room area. I wanted to get his opinion regarding the color of curtains that I should match up with the blinds that I had hung. Well, LaRicko suggested the color that he thought I should go with, which I thought was a great idea as well. And as we sat around and discussed several other things, LaRicko started to nod as if he was getting sleepy. So I said to him, "You need to lie down and take a nap" because he had a dinner date with his future in-laws in a couple of hours as well as a long drive ahead of him to head back to Memphis, but LaRicko assured me that he was fine, and I said "No, you're not getting on the road without the proper rest prior to that drive," and he said again, "Mom, once I'm on the road I'll be fine." But I was determined for him to take a nap. So once I convinced him of that, he decided to lie down, and he asked me to turn the air-conditioning up a little bit because he was a bit warm, so I did and I also placed my new oscillating fan in front of the doorway to make sure he was cool enough. I asked him if that was okay for him, and he said, "Yes, Mom. **I Love you.**" And I said to him, "**I love you too.**" We've always exchanged these three very important words (I love you). So I turned off the light and walked away. Afterward, I decided to run out to the store to pick up the color of curtains that LaRicko suggested so that he could see what they would look like prior to him and his fiancée leaving to head out of town. And so that he could also help me hang them (funny). I returned home after being gone for about an hour or so, and when I walked into the house, I could hear my son snoring as if he was really, really tired,* so I decided to let him continue to rest as I prepared myself to get ready for the dinner appointment with his future in-laws.

When I got to his future in-laws house, I explained to them that LaRicko appeared to have been very tired, and I didn't want to wake him because he needed to be rested up prior to the drive back to Memphis. So I suggested taking my son a plate of food back home with me so at least he'd have dinner. My son's fiancée, her family, and I agreed with that decision, so we all just sat around and enjoyed dinner, laughing and talking.

After spending two hours or so with his fiancée's family, I decided to get back home to wake LaRicko up so that he could eat and get on the road before it was too late in the evening. I didn't want them to have to drive back to Memphis in the dark. **I've always heard if you want to make God laugh, tell him your plans!** So when I got back to the house and walked through the door, I could still hear LaRicko snoring, so I was thinking to myself, oh my goodness, he is really tired. I walked into the kitchen and placed his food in the refrigerator. And then I thought maybe he and his fiancée should wait 'til morning to head home. I walked into the bedroom, and I called LaRicko's name to ask him to turn over and get comfortable because I thought that when a person is snoring while sleeping that they're not in a comfortable position. After calling LaRicko's name a couple of times, I decided to walk over and shake him to wake him up, and he did not respond. So at that point, I became concerned and really started shaking him and calling his name at the same time to get him to wake up, and there was no such luck. So I decided to get a cold wet towel and lay it on his forehead since he appeared to be so warm earlier, but it was so chilly in the house I knew that he'd jump or at least flinch when I placed the cold towel on his forehead. Well, needless to say, he did not even flinch. He was just lying there snoring, but no other response. I picked up the phone and I called my mother and dad because most of the time we feel that parents can fix anything. My mother answered the phone, and I began to explain to her what was going on with my son, and I asked her what she thought I should do next. She immediately said to call 911, and for a minute I thought to myself, my mother can't fix this over the phone, we can fix this with home remedies I'm sure. I wasn't aware of how serious the situation was. "This can't be happening to me," I said. This will be over in a matter of minutes was what I thought. So I did call 911 and explained to the operator what was going on with my son, and the paramedics showed up minutes later. I then picked up the phone and called LaRicko's fiancée to let her know what was going on as well as LaRicko's dad. Minutes later, Chester—LaRicko's dad—and LaRicko's fiancée and her family showed up at my house.

As the paramedics came in, they went into the bedroom where my son was lying helpless. I just couldn't believe that whole thing was happening to us. I stood in the hallway of my house while the police officer began to ask me several questions of what was going on with my son. While standing there talking with the police officer, I heard the paramedic say as well as saw my son's body jerking. "He's having a seizure." At that point, I was just so outdone with what was taking place in front of my eyes. So the paramedic walked out of the bedroom into the hallway where the officer and I were standing and said to me, "We gave him an adrenaline shot because we thought maybe he had taken a drug overdose" **(go figure)**. And usually that type of shot would turn such a condition around, but unfortunately, that wasn't the case for my son. The paramedics had to take LaRicko to the hospital because *what was going on with my son was more serious than the paramedics expected. Can you imagine how I was feeling at that point? That was one of the happiest days of my life—the earlier part of the day—and then it went downhill.*

The paramedics prepared LaRicko to be taken to the hospital, and as they put his lifeless-looking body on the stretcher, I began looking at the healthy-looking person that was happy as ever the earlier part of the day, expecting all good things to happen for him and his fiancée in a matter of months, and things just took a turn for the worse. I just couldn't understand what was going on and why, and as I prayed to the Lord on my way to the hospital, I couldn't help but remember

Proverbs 3:5-6, which says "Trust in the Lord with all thine heart; and lean not unto thine own understanding. In all thy ways acknowledge him, and he shall direct thy path."

Well, at that area in my life, I really needed the Lord to direct my path because I'd never experienced anything that severe in my life. I'd dealt with crisis before that money could fix, but at that point, all the money in the world couldn't change that one.

After my son's father and I finally made it to the hospital, we had to go to the emergency room to find out where they had taken our son. The nurse came out and directed us to the little waiting room area where we had to wait until the doctor came out to let us know what was going on with LaRicko. When the doctor came out the first time, he said to me that it had appeared that LaRicko had a stroke because the entire right side of his body seemed to have been paralyzed. My mouth flew open.

"What?" And the doctor said to me that they would continue to run tests on LaRicko to see if there could have been something else going on that could have been missed. Minutes later, the doctor returned and said that the test results possibly were indicating that my son had an aneurysm. I sat in my seat, saying to myself, Lord you said you will never put more on me than I can bare, but things were beginning to feel almost unbearable. But the doctor told me that the staff was still running more tests, and as the results came to him, the doctor would come out and let us know the findings. I began to sit there looking around at the walls, asking the Lord what I had done to be in a situation like that. Well, as the time went on that night, the doctor came back in the room to let us know that the results were beginning to point toward LaRicko having meningitis. Of course, you could only imagine what was going through my mind around that point of the evening. And when the doctor came back with his final findings, the doctor said that LaRicko had a seizure in his sleep and no oxygen had gotten to my son's brain for over four minutes, which caused LaRicko to be completely brain-dead. I said, "What?" I rushed to my phone, and I called and told my mother and father what the doctor said regarding my son's final diagnosis. They both were in total disbelief. I remember my mother's exact words. She said, "Well, if that doesn't just beat all!" Afterward, I called my brothers to let them know what was going on with LaRicko as well. My brothers were in complete shock! Especially to think that LaRicko just came up for a weekend to St. Louis to visit, and then he's pronounced to be completely brain-dead. I called my best friend and a coworker to let them know what was going on, and to my surprise, my coworker came up to the hospital and stayed with us most of the night. My best friend and her mother showed up shortly after that to be with us also. They all sat with us while the doctor kept going back and forth, checking my son over to see if there was something else that they could possibly be missing. But in the meantime, the doctor saw

that the condition that LaRicko was in was not going to be a quick fix, so the staff admitted LaRicko into the hospital and placed him in the intensive care unit.

We sat for hours upon hours, waiting to see if LaRicko was going to respond. I went into the room and tried to get my son to respond to me as I looked at his lifeless-looking body. I'd pray while I was standing there, asking the Lord to please show up for me. I couldn't believe that I was going to lose my son so soon; he was only twenty-six years old. I couldn't see that happening to me. I began to think back on different things that happened to me years ago regarding LaRicko. After the birth of my son, I would always say to my mother, "I wish that I never had a baby." And my mother would always remind me to be careful of the words that I'd speak. But at that time, I did not realize that my tongue was a weapon, and I felt that I meant every word that I was saying, so it didn't matter to me at the time anyway. Mom would keep reminding to be careful of what I was saying, but yet I didn't take her seriously. So as I stood there looking down at my son, I couldn't help but be reminded of when LaRicko was four months old, and I had gone out of town for my aunt's funeral in Arkansas and I left LaRicko with his dad. Chester and I had purchased LaRicko's milk formula from one of our neighborhood stores. And while I was out of town, Chester fed LaRicko with that formula. And, needless to say, when I got back into town, as the week went on, LaRicko began to cry constantly. I tried to pamper him as a mother would, but he continued to cry. I tried to give my son his formula, and as I'd begin to do that, LaRicko would vomit it up all over himself and me. And as the time went on, my son had begun to develop diarrhea. And I didn't know what was going on with him. So I picked up the phone and called the doctor to ask questions regarding my baby's symptoms, and the doctor right away told me to bring him to the office so LaRicko could be examined. So Chester and I rushed LaRicko over to the doctor's office. Once the doctor examined our son, we found that he was dehydrated and that if I'd waited much longer before I'd brought him in, we could have lost him. The doctor sent us straight over to the hospital with my son where they immediately admitted my baby into the hospital. When the doctor showed up later at the hospital and came in to talk to us, sharing with Chester and I that they were having a very hard time trying to find a vein in LaRicko's almost-lifeless body to begin an IV because he was so dehydrated, I felt so sad and began to think about the past comments I had made regarding not wanting a child. We did not realize the severity of LaRicko's condition until the doctor came out and told us how dehydrated he was. The doctor began to question us regarding what we'd been feeding him. And as we pondered about it, we traced the issue back to the formula that we'd purchased from the neighborhood store to find that the due date on the can of the formula had expired almost a year ago, to our surprise. But God's grace to a mother's prayer kept us. I thank God every day for my mother's and father's prayers.

Not only did I almost lose my son once, there was another incident one Mother's Day. Again I'd gone out of town for the weekend to visit with my parents on Mother's Day, and I remember that my spirit that week was not at all at ease. I wanted to go to Arkansas, but at the same time, I didn't feel at all comfortable about the idea. But at the time, LaRicko's Aunt Lela kept on me to go to Arkansas with her, so reluctantly; I packed my bags and prepared for the trip. I spoke with LaRicko prior to my leaving, sharing with him that I'd be back in town on Sunday, which would actually be on Mother's Day, and I at least would like to see my son on that day when I got back, and LaRicko assured me that he'd be here when I got back. The weekend was great. I enjoyed spending quality time with my parents. I enjoyed just being home with my dad and mom. I went over and visited with my grandmother also. It was just an awesome weekend, but on the inside, my spirit just did not allow me to relax for some reason.

On Sunday morning as we prepared to head back to St. Louis, I tried to call LaRicko, but I was not fortunate to get in touch with him prior to him leaving for work that morning. But once I got back to St. Louis that evening, I tried to contact LaRicko again, still with no such luck, thinking to myself this was pretty unusual for him not to have tried to contact me. After a while, I called his girlfriend to ask her if she'd heard from LaRicko, and she shared with me that once he got off from his job, he and his brother had gone to take their dogs out to the park to take them for a walk. So I began to try and contact his brother, and again, I had no such luck. So of course at this point, I'd begun to worry. After a few more hours of waiting to hear from my son, I finally received a call from his girlfriend to inform me that my son was at a hospital. I was in shock. "What do you mean 'in the hospital'?" I asked. She shared with me that as LaRicko and his brother were leaving the park, LaRicko was sitting in the back of the truck that his brother was driving, securing the dogs, when his brother decided to make a quick U-turn in the middle of a very busy street, catching LaRicko completely off guard, throwing him off the back of the truck. When LaRicko hit the ground, he was knocked unconscious. I thanked God that the people that was in the car behind them saw my son lying there on the ground, and one of the young ladies got out of the car, called 911, and guided oncoming traffic around my son until the ambulance got there to take him to the hospital. I could not believe what I was hearing. So needless to say, my son spent Mother's Day in the hospital. And as the time went and I got the opportunity to go and see my son, at the sight of him, being that he was so banged up with cuts and bruises, I was really upset, but in my mind and heart, I thanked God for LaRicko being alive. We were so blessed that it wasn't any worse than that. So with those things going through my mind, I began asking the Lord why was it that the enemy had tried to take my son's life on several occasions. I know in the beginning of his life, when I was much younger and didn't know any better, I was speaking foolish things; but since then, I've learned better so I'm doing better, and I was looking forward to a great future for me and my son. I was looking forward to seeing him get married and looking forward to my grandbabies. But there we were again, at the hospital, praying for my son's life.

I walked back to the intensive care waiting room area where I had several friends there waiting along with Chester, my son's father. Shortly afterward, LaRicko's brother came to the hospital with a friend of his. And we all had begun to sit around that first night just praying for LaRicko to overcome that condition.

As the next morning came, we had several doctors and nurses coming out to discuss with us what their thoughts were regarding LaRicko's condition. And as time went on that day, I kept praying that things would change for the better. The doctor walked out and called me to the corner of the intensive care unit hallway, and he said to me, "I'm really sorry, but your son will never come back because his brain is completely dead." As I'd said in the earlier part of my journal, the doctor described LaRicko as a car without a motor. As the doctor said, my son's brain was like an egg if you were to fry it in a skillet. The doctor made it clear to me that my son's condition was never going to change, so I needed to let the staff at the hospital know when I wanted to unplug LaRicko, and they gave me a week to make that decision. I thanked the doctor for *his services, and I told him that I'd let him know when I had decided to unplug my son.*

*So at that point, I just wanted to call my pastor so that he could come and pray us out of that situation. I didn't know where else to turn. So I called my church to speak with my pastor, and of all times, my pastor was still on vacation. How dare he take a vacation in the middle of my crisis! I thought to myself, as if my pastor could have known that it was going to happen to us. I couldn't believe that, just when I'm having a crisis. So I began to pray, and in the midst of my praying, it came to me that the Lord said in his Word in the book of **Joshua 1:5 that says,***

"I will be with thee: I will not fail thee, nor forsake thee,"

so with that in my mind and heart, I knew I wasn't alone. Being that my pastor wasn't there, I spoke with one of the other ministers at the church who asked me to go into the intensive unit while speaking to him on the phone, and the minister asked me to lay my hands on my son as he prayed for him. I thanked him for his prayers and hung up the phone. As I looked down on my son, I was still in disbelief.

As that week went on, as I said earlier in the journal, I walked into my son's room, and the nurse was standing there working with his IV tubes and blood pressure. I was happy to see someone in LaRicko's room working with him, which gave me some kind of feeling of hope, being that they'd already declared him brain-dead. When I entered the room, I spoke to the nurse and asked, "How are you doing?" She said, "Fine," so I asked, "How's my son doing today?" and she answered, saying, "The same." And I asked, "So no changes at all . . . ?" I'll never forget how the nurse stopped and looked at me as if she was calling me an idiot, and she said, "Be realistic, he's not going to make it out of here!" You couldn't imagine how I felt as a mother for such an uncaring person to be the one who was working on my son. Afterward, I said to her, "Thank you for caring over my son," and I walked over and sat down by LaRicko's bedside and began to talk to him and pray as well. I prayed and asked the Lord to please send a caring and prayerful person to us because it was hard enough as it was besides having such a negative person to deal with. We knew that God does answer prayers. I had begun to pray as it is written in the book of **Psalm 143:1:**

"Hear my prayer, O Lord, give ear to my supplications: in thy faithfulness answer me, and in thy righteousness."

So when the next day came, the nurse that was caring for my son was such a sweet person; as I talked with her regarding LaRicko, she said to me, "Just continue to pray because God can do anything, even if they are saying that your son's brain is dead, just keep the faith." And I thanked God for finally sending a positive person to us. So as that week went on, my son was still lying there in a coma. And at that point, we just continued to pray for LaRicko's recovery.

Later on that afternoon, my daughter in-law Gwen, who is married to my stepson, came to the hospital and brought my grandbabies, and I thought it was so sweet of her as she always was. Gwen had bought me a prayer locket, which was something that I'd never seen before. It was a silver necklace with a charm on it, which was shaped like a Bible. What was so interesting about that locket was you were suppose to open it and pray while it was open and then close it up and wait for *your prayers to be answered. Well, I opened the Bible locket, and Gwen, my grandbabies, and I begun to pray for LaRicko's healing, and then I closed it up. Then Gwen took the necklace and placed it around my neck, and I felt so confident at that point that everything was going to be just fine. My grandbabies kept saying, "Granny Diane, Uncle Ricko is going to be okay." And of course, that made me feel so good to know that my babies could be so positive after seeing their uncle Ricko in such a terrible-looking condition.*

Well, on that Sunday while I was sitting there in the intensive care unit working on a crossword puzzle book, my cousin came up to see my son and I, and after she visited with us for a while, she wanted to take me out for dinner at Red Lobster's, and of course I didn't have an appetite such as that, but she didn't take no for an answer. I never wanted to leave the hospital because I felt that I needed to be there with my son at all times, but I went reluctantly. So after we went over and had dinner, which was a nice getaway for me, but my mind was on my son the whole time. So when my cousin dropped me off back at the hospital and I went back to the intensive care unit to check on my son, the doctor was there waiting because he needed to speak with me regarding doing a tracheotomy in LaRicko's throat, which meant that they had to cut his throat and place a tube in it because at that point the tube was going through LaRicko's mouth, which the doctor said would cause an infection if it continued like that too long. So of course I was okay with that so that my son would not get an infection because we had enough issues that we were dealing with already. Well, after I agreed to allow the procedure to be done, the doctor set it up for the next day.

So I went back out to the waiting area where I begun to work on my crossword puzzle again. Shortly afterward, I received a call on my cell *phone to inform me that LaRicko's brother and my grandson had been in a motorcycle accident, and they were being brought to the emergency room down the hall from where I was sitting. In disbelief, I was just speechless. But I said to the Lord, "You are in control. Just give me the strength that I need to handle all these issues that are attacking us." Later on, LaRicko's dad came up to the hospital, and I began to tell him that he needed to pray and ask the Lord what message that he needed to get from this. It was a sad time for his dad's family because two weekends ago, Chester's family had their Mom's funeral, and the next Sunday, LaRicko was hospitalized and being pronounced brain-dead, and the following Sunday, Chester's son Michael and grandson were in a motorcycle accident. I just felt that God was trying to get Chester's attention as well. Things appeared to be spinning out of control.*

My family—Mother, Father, and three brothers along with my nephew Tony and several cousins—came from afar to see LaRicko for themselves, being that it sounded unbelievable. I remember when Tony went in to see LaRicko as he was lying there in a coma, LaRicko opened his eyes, and it appeared that LaRicko was staring at Tony. My son's eyes were following Tony as he began to walk back and forth in the hospital room. Tony began to talk to LaRicko, saying, "Do you want me to stay here with you?" He felt that my son was trying to tell him not to leave him. Afterward, my nephew walked over to my son's bedside and assured him that he wasn't going to leave him. And after a while, my nephew and I went out to the waiting area where the rest of my family members had gathered as they all sat around and continued to try and grasp what was really going on.

The doctor that was caring for my son at that time walked up and asked if she could speak to me in private. Of course I agreed. The doctor said to me that they had given LaRicko a week at the hospital and he had not responded at all, and she included that the hospital couldn't keep my son there much longer, being that he was completely brain-dead. She also included that no other facility would take my son other than a nursing home, and I needed to decide which nursing home I wanted to release LaRicko to because they couldn't continue to keep him at their facility. Things were really beginning to get too tough for me being that I've seen how people have not been cared for properly at nursing homes, and at the same time, I didn't feel that my son needed to go to a nursing home; I felt that he needed to be transferred to a rehabilitation facility. I knew that my request sounded crazy to the doctor being that LaRicko was in a coma and was diagnosed completely brain-dead, but I felt in my heart that my son was going to be okay after a while. But the doctors said there was no way that LaRicko was going to come out of the vegetated state that he was in. "Your son is a vegetable," the doctor said, "and he would remain that way until he expired." So that afternoon, my son's brother was taken into surgery and was there for quite some time, and while he was in surgery, the staff had begun prepping LaRicko to go in the exact surgery room right behind his brother so that they can perform the tracheotomy on him. Was it praying time or what? And at that moment, I really needed to know what to do next. I was so numb at that area of my issues, I didn't know what to think or feel. But the doctors said to me that the procedure that was going to be performed on my son would be much better for him being that the tube that was going through his mouth would cause infection because it had been there for over a week. So of course I was just going with the flow of things, taking it one day at a time. I was praying hard all the way for the Lord to order my steps.

On that Monday, some of my coworkers came out to the hospital to see my son and me. And to their surprise, he was in a much worse condition than they thought. I thought it was so nice of the people in my job to have brought LaRicko and me beautiful cards as well as them taking up a collection for us, which I thought was such a blessing. I remember two of the young ladies who worked with me, Ronnae and Lachelle, who were always so comical. Both of them had begun to tease LaRicko as they stood beside his sick bed. They kept leaning over him, saying, "LaRicko, you really don't have to get married, so you can stop playing games now!" They would always lift my spirits no matter what was going on. Ronnae and Lachelle were saying from the very beginning when I first shared with them that my son was going to get married and what the wedding plans were, the two of them would say that LaRicko really didn't want to get married, and we'd always chuckle behind that statement. So after LaRicko had gotten ill, Ronnae and Lachelle began to say that he's just trying to get out of the wedding plans, which was scheduled for August 23.

Another one of the guys that I've always referred to him as my play son called me and said, "Mom, don't worry about LaRicko, he's just faking." My play son continued with "LaRicko's just jealous of me because you refer to me as your play son. LaRicko is just trying to get special attention from you," he said. My play son continued talking while I (Mom) was sitting out in the waiting room. LaRicko was probably in the intensive care unit laughing and walking around watching out for me (Mom) so that he can get back in the bed before I see him. So as you can see, I had several comedians in my life to keep me smiling.

As that week went on, my stepson's aunt was so sweet to send her daughter to the hospital to see LaRicko and me, along with a beautiful teddy bear and a large baby bottle that was a bank, and she had placed money in it as well. As the baby bottle bank sat around in the waiting area of the hospital, people began to place money in it. I thought this was so thoughtful of his aunt to do such a thing. She did the same thing for LaRicko's brother who was in the motorcycle accident. She also sent a message too by her daughter to let me know that she was praying for us. This also made me feel so good to know that total strangers were praying with us.

Chapter 2

Hearing and Recognizing the Lord's Voice

*A*s *I looked back over that whole situation, I'd get a nervous feeling inside, and with that in mind, I knew that it was the Lord who was carrying me. I remembered when I'd always pray and ask the Lord to allow me to date and marry a minister or to marry someone who was serious about the Word of God because I always felt that I needed that to help me to draw closer to the Lord, but through this walk, the Lord showed me that I don't need men—I only needed the Lord.*

Well, as the days went on, while I continued my spiritual walk, I still wasn't getting any responses from my son; he was just lying there with *a cold white towel on his forehead, flat on his back with his hands just lying across his body, tubes all over his body and on a ventilator, which kept him alive. After days of the same condition with my son, I kept getting comments from the nurses: LaRicko was not getting any better. But I'd continue to go into my son's room and pray at his bedside. Each day as I went into LaRicko's room, I'd repeat the **twenty-third psalm:***

"The Lord is my shepherd, I shall not want. He maketh me to lie down in green pastures: he leadeth me beside the still waters. He restoreth my soul: he leadeth me in the path of righteousness for his name sake. Yea, though I walk through the valley of the shadow of death, I will fear no evil: for thou art with me; thy rod and thy staff they comfort me. Thou preparest a table before me in the presence of mine enemies: thou anointest my head with oil; my cup runneth over. Surely goodness and mercy shall follow me all the days of my life: and I will dwell in the house of the Lord forever. Amen!"

*And when I'd get to the fourth verse, I'd say to my son "As we walk through this situation, we're not going to stay here, we are not going to fear anything that we were facing because the Lord is with us, and he's going to bring us out of this." I also reminded him how much he and I use to talk about how important it was to have faith. I'd explain to him that as long as we had the faith at least the size of a grain of a mustard seed as found in the book of **Luke 17:6:***

"And the Lord said, If ye had faith as a grain of mustard seed, ye might say unto this sycamine tree, Be thou plucked up by the root, and be thou planted in the sea; and it should obey you."

And I knew that my son had at least that much faith because I had always instilled that in him. So as I prayed, I trusted that my son believed with me that we were going to come out of that situation. As the time went on, the intensive care waiting area continued to flood with friends and relatives. We had so many people there at all times of the day. And I felt so much better while the crowd was around. I had so much love and support shown to me those first few days, and I was appreciating all that. Different loved ones and friends would go in the unit and see my son, and they'd come out crying as if they'd viewed a dead body. The intensive care unit was flooded with people; some prayed with me, and others were there as spectators. Through it all, I continued to be strong because I never felt at any point that it was over for my son.

I remember when I started to hunger for the Word of God. I wanted to be able to feel his presence as well as to recognize when the Lord was speaking to me. I'd say, "Lord, help me to recognize you and when you're speaking to me." I just felt I wasn't reaching him in that area of my life. But I continued to pray for that anointing, and through what I was experiencing, I really needed to recognize the Lord when he's speaking so that I would know what to do for LaRicko next. So as I took that walk, my friend came out and prayed for LaRicko, and afterward, my friend told me that he and I were going to fast and pray for a few days, and that's what we did. And as the days went on with the fasting and praying, I didn't feel at that point that I needed to unplug my son. I was so sure that the feelings came through my fasting and praying.

Later that evening, a friend of the family who was a minister was traveling through St. Louis when he had heard about LaRicko's unfortunate condition. The friend and his little son came to the hospital to see LaRicko, and the minister and his son shared with us that they were going to keep LaRicko in their prayers. What I thought was very impressive was the friend asked for us to all grab hands so that we could pray for LaRicko's healing, and he said that his little son was going to do the praying. That little boy was about five or six years old, and he prayed from his heart. I asked his dad, "Does he pray like this all the time?" and his dad said yes. He shared with me that his son has actually preached a sermon before. "Oh my goodness," I said as I began to hug the little boy. This was truly overwhelming.

The doctor came to me a couple days later and said, "We really need you to go ahead and make a decision to unplug your son because his condition is not going to change. LaRicko is completely brain-dead, and there is no cure for that." So I asked the doctor if I could have a second opinion. And the doctor said to me, "I will go back and see who I can get to agree to give you a second opinion because the first doctor that confirmed that he was completely brain-dead is one of our best top neurologists of this hospital." But the doctor included that she would at least check and see if there's anyone that would agree to evaluate LaRicko to assure that he was completely brain-dead.

While I was sitting there conversing with different people in the waiting area, a nurse came out and asked if she could speak with me. Of course I was waiting on something positive to finally come my way, but instead, the nurse said to me that the doctor sent her out to inform me that if I chose to get a second-opinion doctor for my son, the present doctor at that point would no longer be the doctor for my son. I was in complete shock! "Why wouldn't anyone be allowed the opportunity to get a second opinion over someone's life?" I asked. We were speaking of a human here, and that human happened to be my son—and I couldn't *get a second opinion? And the nurse said to me, "no". So at that point, I didn't need a doctor like that anyway! So I thanked the nurse as I walked back to my seat and sat down, and I began to pray for the Lord to just order my steps because I just didn't know what else to do.*

Order my steps in thy word: and let not any iniquity have dominion over me. (Psalm 119:133)

I just pleaded to the Lord to make the situation all better. I just couldn't see giving up my son like that. I said to the Lord, "LaRicko is my only child, and I don't want to lose him. LaRicko is all I have." I did not want to give up on him like that. I just could not see myself not being a mother anymore. As I sat there praying, it came to me.

For God so loved the world, that he gave his only begotten Son, that whosoever believeth in him should no perish, but have everlasting life. (John 3:16)

So at that area of my request, I knew I needed to come with something stronger than that because if the Lord gave up his son, what would have made me think I was any better than that? And I continued to pray and ask the Lord for the right words to pray. So after a while, the nurse finally came back out to the waiting area to speak to me once again, and she informed me that a doctor came forth and agreed to examine LaRicko and give us a second opinion. I was so happy and thanked God for the doctor that gave us a chance. I prayed that the Lord would give me a sign through those test results from the second-opinion doctor to give me the knowledge whether to hold on to LaRicko or let him go.

After examining LaRicko for hours, the doctor came out and said to me that he only wanted to speak to me and my son's father. So Chester, the doctor, and I proceeded back to the intensive care unit where our son was lying there in a coma, and the doctor said to us he was not trying to give us false hope because our son's brain was severely damaged. He included that LaRicko's brain was not completely dead, but it was so severely damaged that he didn't want us to think that our son would get any better. Believe it or not, I was so happy to hear that because I prayed for the Lord to give me a sign, and just what I prayed for was answered for me. I felt that the information was enough for me to hold on to LaRicko a while longer. In my mind, there was a difference between LaRicko having a severely damaged brain than LaRicko being completely brain-dead; I felt that at that point, I at least had a chance for him to get better.

Another day passed, and LaRicko had begun to open his eyes, and I'll never forget how bloodshot his eyes were. The nurse said to me that it was because LaRicko's eyes had been closed for so many days. As I watched him, LaRicko just stared straight ahead. I'd wave my hands in front of his eyes to see if he'd notice them or blink, but unfortunately, nothing happened. I began to place my hands under his hands, and I asked him to press down on my hands, and he'd press down as if he was following my command, and I was excited about LaRicko's responses, and I couldn't wait to share that with the doctor. After the doctor came into LaRicko's room, I shared with him what my son had done, but the doctor explained to me that the body does all kinds of reflexes when it's dead. The doctor also included that all I was getting from my son were simply body reflexes. I was very disappointed to hear that because I was hoping that LaRicko was finally coming around. Unfortunately, the doctor said, *"No, LaRicko is still in a coma, so he is not even hearing you."*

*One day while I was sitting in the intensive care waiting area, a minister from the church that we attend walked up to me. That minister was also a neighbor from years ago who used to come over and visit with us even before LaRicko was born. When I looked up and saw his face, I was so happy; he hugged me and said, "Diane, tell me what's going on." So I began to explain to the minister what happened to LaRicko. Afterward, I shared with the minister what the doctors' diagnosis was. I told him that the results from the doctors were saying that my son was completely brain-dead and there'd be absolutely no changes in LaRicko's condition. That minister really touched my heart because after we talked, he began to pray with me, and he also gave me some healing scriptures, and then he said, "Let's go back and see Ricko." So we took a walk back into the intensive care unit area, and the minister looked down at LaRicko, and he said, "Let's place our hands on LaRicko as we pray for him," and the minister prayed out of his heart for my son. After the prayer, the minister said to me, "Well, we are going to wait on the Lord. Let's just trust God on this, and it will all be okay." But what I admired so much about the minister was when I told him what the doctors said about what was going on with my son; he shook his head as if to say they're wrong. That's what I needed, someone to agree with my faith as well as my prayers, and that minister appeared to be the one. I never wanted anyone to agree with me just because they knew me or felt sorry for me; I needed someone to have faith, and I truly felt that this particular minister was the one. As I thought back on years ago, I would have never thought of him becoming a minister **(God is truly amazing).** And to see him now with me in my crisis . . . you just never know why people are placed in your life. That minister is truly an anointed man!*

After the minister left the hospital, I'd begun to read the healing scriptures that he had given me, not understanding (lean not to your own understanding, but in all my ways; acknowledge him, and he will direct your path) what I was reading, but I began to pray and ask God to help me to understand those scriptures.

Trust in the Lord with all thine heart; and lean not unto thine own understanding. In all thy ways acknowledge him, and he shall direct thy path. (Proverbs 3:5-6)

*I remembered very well one of the scriptures that really had me puzzled, which was found in the book of **Isaiah 53:5**:*

"But he was wounded for our transgressions, he was bruised for our iniquities: the chastisement of our peace was upon him; and with his stripes we are healed."

I read that scripture over and over and just couldn't grasp the clear understanding of it. But I prayed that God would make it plain for me. Through my walk with the Lord, I truly understand that scripture now.

The intensive care unit was still overly crowded with so many people there for their loved ones also. I remembered these two sisters coming over to me and sharing with me how sick their mother was at that time, and they were here from out of town to be with her. They asked me who was I there with, and I said, "My son," and I began to share my situation with the two of them. They both expressed how sorry they were to hear about my son's condition\ and told me that they would pray for me as well as I would pray with them for their mother. They also *included that they had a prayer cloth with blessed oil on it, and they'd been praying for their mother and wished that they had an extra cloth to share with me, but I said, "Just continue to pray with us because it's the prayers that we need." So we all prayed together and trusted God on our outcome. Each day that those two sisters would come out to the hospital, they would come over to check on me and my son, which I thought was very considerate of them, being that they were in the middle of their own crisis. On that Sunday afternoon, these two sisters came over to me and said, "Well, Mamma has gone on to heaven now, and she's not in anymore pain. We will continue to pray for you and your son." Afterward, we embraced each other with hugs, and the one sister who had the prayer cloth passed it on to me. She said, "My mother was old and has lived her life and is blessed to be out of her pain, but your son is young and will be fine. Just hang in there, he will be okay." I appreciated those positive words coming from total strangers; it sounded like faith speaking to me.*

When I went back to see how my son was doing, the nurse decided to reduce LaRicko's sedation medication to see how he'd respond, and as LaRicko was coming down off the sedation medication, he really appeared to be responding to us. My son also had a frown on his face as if he was in some type of pain. And there again when I complained about him being in pain, I heard the same thing over and over again, that LaRicko was brain-dead and that he couldn't possibly be aware of any pain. So as that day went on, I was a bit disappointed because I felt that my son needed some relief from the pain he appeared to be having.

Being at that point of LaRicko's condition and I still hadn't given the doctors a date to unplug my son, they were actually ready for us to leave the hospital. I just didn't know what to do. I began to do my usual *praying, asking the Lord to order my steps because I didn't know what to do, and the doctors actually were getting tired of us being there since I hadn't given them an actual date to unplug LaRicko. Fortunately the doctor ordered a pain patch to be placed on my son's left arm, being that I complained that LaRicko appeared to be having pain on the left side of his body. I'm sure that was done just to satisfy me, but I at least felt better about that. A friend of mine that actually worked in the hospital would come and check on us every day. One day when my friend came up to see us, I explained to her that the doctors wanted my son moved out of their facility right away to a nursing home and that LaRicko was in no condition to leave the hospital. And of course, I did not want him in a nursing home. I felt that would truly be the last of my son if I placed him in a nursing home. After hearing my situation, my friend said, "I'm going to speak with this doctor on the floor that I actually work on to see if the doctor would take your son on as his patient, who would give you more time to see if LaRicko would recover." **People are in our lives for reasons!** I thanked my friend as she walked away to check with that doctor for me.*

*My friend returned later that day and said that doctor was more than happy to do that for us. Once again, God had shown up. She said the doctor would be up later to speak with me, and believe it or not, shortly afterward, that doctor came up and went back to the intensive care unit and examined LaRicko, and shortly afterward, the doctor came back to the waiting area where I was sitting and spoke with me to inform me that he was going to be my son's doctor from that point on. I thanked him for giving us that opportunity. **Praise the Lord!***

It was not long after that when the nurse came out to inform me that they were preparing my son to leave the intensive care unit to be placed on another floor so that the new doctor can care for him from that point on.

I was excited on one hand because LaRicko was at least going to be out of the intensive care unit; that was truly a blessing! God had shown up once again! But on the other hand, I wanted to be doing the right thing by trying to keep my son in the hospital rather than a nursing home. So I prayed, "Lord, continue to order my steps."

Later that afternoon, I heard Minister Mullins coming down the hall; there was something about his footsteps that I could just recognize him when I'd hear them. He was so supportive in his prayers as well as showing up at the hospital all the time. Each time Minister Mullins came to the hospital, he'd go in and pray for my son, and every time he'd leave, he'd look at LaRicko and say, "I'll be back, I haven't given up, just keep the faith," and that would encourage me even more.

Well, the staff told me to gather all my son's personal items because we were getting ready to go down to another floor at the hospital. As I was doing that, I was still praying for the Lord to order my steps because I needed to hear from him and recognize the Lord's voice when he's speaking to me. The weight was getting heavier and heavier because I knew at some point; I was not going to have an option to keep LaRicko there or to leave. **Lord, I need you now!**

Once we got down to the next floor, the nurses began to introduce themselves to let us know who's going to be working with my son for the rest of that day. I'll never forget the first nurse that worked with my son. She felt so sad for me as the mother, and because she knew that my son would never respond to me again, she gave me a hug. I told her I was expecting my first grandchild and that he was suppose to have been getting married that month of August, and the nurse really was sorry because she said that my son would never get to know his first child nor will he ever get married. She said to me, "Just continue to pray for him because there's nothing like a mothers' prayer."

On the second day of my son being out of the intensive care unit, it started to be a really bad day for us. LaRicko's temperature was starting to elevate higher and higher. By midday, his temperature had elevated up to 102 degrees. The staff kept trying to get his temperature down, but they were not successful; as a matter of fact, it elevated more. As the day went on, I questioned the nurse to see if any of my son's medication had been changed since he had left the ICU, and the nurse said yes; she continued with "But that's not the reason your son's temperature was elevated." She explained to me that there's something in the back of the brain called a splint, and it controls the body temperature, and when a person is brain-dead, the splint cannot control the body temperature; it's no longer functional. The nurse also included that the temperature would continue to elevate until my son expires. So after the nurse left the room, I began to say to my son, "As we walk through the valley, we are not going to stay here, we know that the Lord is with us, so with that in mind we want fear no evil, because the Lord is truly with us" **(Psalm 23:4)!**

Chapter 3

My Faith Being Tested by God

*H*ere we were once again to a worse stage of LaRicko's condition. I just could not believe we didn't have a solution for what was going on in our life. My son's temperature was getting worse by the hour. I asked the nurse again if they would just check and see if it could possibly be the change in medication, and I was assured by the nurse that it was not the medication. I was praying and trusting God to work that out for me because I just didn't know what to do. I needed the Lord's guidance on that one. I felt so lost! So as I sat there talking to my son, the nurse began to check his blood pressure and temperature, and she talked to me mother to mother, and she said, "I know it's going to be hard to lose your son, but there are times when we have to just let go." She continued with "You don't want to watch

LaRicko suffer, that would make it harder for you to just watch him deteriorate day after day."

As I listened to her, I felt so lost because she was right about the fact that I didn't want to watch LaRicko suffer, but at the same time, I kept saying if anybody were to fight and try to save a child, it would be Momma. I prayed so hard to the Lord and asked him to show me what I needed to do. I'd included in my prayers how I knew God is a miracle worker, and I knew he healed a woman who had an issue of blood found in the book of **Matthew 9:20-21:**

"And, behold, a woman, which was diseased with an issue of blood twelve years, came behind him, touched the hem of his garment: For she said within herself, If I may touch his garment, I shall be whole."

And with the woman having the faith that she had, the Lord made her whole again. I knew I had faith, and my son was in no condition at that time to trust and have the faith with me, so I prayed to the Lord. I knew if God did it for the woman in the Bible, I knew the Lord would do it for us. I went on to say the Lord fed five thousand men plus women and children with two fish and five loaves, which is found in the book of **Matthew 14:17-21:**

"And they say unto him, We have here but five loaves, and two fishes. He said, 'Bring them hither to me.' And he commanded the multitude to sit down on the grass, and took the five loaves, and the two fishes, and looking up to heaven, he blessed, and break, and gave the loaves to his disciples, and the disciples to the multitude. And they did all eat, and were filled: and they took up of the fragments that

remained twelve baskets full. And they that had eaten were about five thousand men, beside women and children."

So I continued with "If the Lord can perform a miracle such as that, I know he can bring my son back from the brain-dead condition." And every time I'd speak to someone regarding LaRicko, I'd say, "He's going to be okay," and add that it's just going to take some time. I'd always get strange looks from most of the people that I was talking with as to imply that I must have been losing my mind! They'd look at me as to say there was no way that someone in LaRicko's condition was going to come out of that alive, but I felt I had the faith to walk that road.

The night was a really long night! LaRicko did not close his eyes all night long. He appeared to be staring at something, and he had start kicking out of control. And nevertheless, his temperature kept elevating, and his blood pressure was not coming down at all. I was beginning to question my own faith and couldn't figure out if I was holding on to my son as a mother would or if that was the faith that I had to trust God that he was going to work it out for us. As in chapter 2**, I needed to recognize the Lord's voice as well as know if my faith is being tested.** As LaRicko's condition continued throughout the night, I was so exhausted physically as well as mentally.

When that next morning came, things hadn't changed very much as far as LaRicko's kicking out of control, temperature, and blood pressure elevating. And then other issues had begun to come up. The nurse and medical technician came in my son's room all through the night getting blood from him to try and determine what else was going on with LaRicko. Well, in the afternoon of the next day, the doctor entered my son's room and said to me that it looked as if LaRicko had blood clots *forming in his legs. Wow! Things were just continuing to head in the wrong direction for us. I said, "Lord, you said you'd be here for me. I don't hear you, I don't know what to do anymore," but it came to me in my spirit right away. Don't claim blood clots in LaRicko's legs, his legs are okay. And as I stood by LaRicko's bedside and looked at him, I said, "You don't have any blood clots in your legs. Your legs are just fine." I trusted God to make that right. I stood at the end of my son's bed as I continued to pray while LaRicko was kicking his legs out of control. A voice spoke to me again and said, "Place your hands at the bottom of each foot and press toward him and allow him to push back, and that would be therapy for LaRicko to keep the strength in his legs strong." And as I began to do that and encouraged him to continue to kick back, I felt much better about that condition that he was going through. There's times when we have to take what appears to be a bad situation and make the best of it.*

The very next day, we started out with the same issues; things just weren't getting any better on either one of LaRicko's conditions, and my son was looking even worse. Later on as that day passed, being that the procedures the staff was using weren't successful in getting his blood pressure to come down below stroke level without medication, the doctor decided to start LaRicko on blood pressure medication. I just did not believe what I was hearing. But the nurses felt that the temperature was just going to be with him until he expired, being that the splint in his brain was destroyed, but I didn't feel that at all. I continued to be persistent with the fact that they were giving him some medication that was not agreeing with his system. So as the nurses would come in and out of the room evaluating my son's situation, I'd always bring that subject up (regarding the medication not agreeing with my son's system). And of course, no one listened to me. Go figure!

Later on that evening, the doctor ordered the staff to bring in a bed of ice so that LaRicko could be placed on it because his temperature was unbelievable. So they came in with the ice bed and placed my son on it. I couldn't believe that my son was actually lying on a bed of ice. It was freezing, but the staff informed me that this was the only way to keep my son's body cool because the temperature wasn't going down, and LaRicko appeared to be very irritated. And that continued for several days. It was getting harder and harder for me to see his body just transform into an unbelievable state. He appeared to be losing weight by the day. His hands were continuing to retract under. When his fiancée and I would come in each day, we would put LaRicko's socks and tennis shoes on his feet to try and keep his feet from dropping because if his feet dropped, I was told that there's no way he'd ever walk again. So with that in mind, his fiancée and I would always make sure that this was done daily even though the doctor had said that LaRicko was completely brain-dead; as you can see here, we were holding on to our faith.

After about a week of my son's challenging temperature as well as his blood pressure continuing to spiral out of control, the doctor finally decided to bring an infections specialist on the scene to see if the specialist could find out what was actually going on with my son in those areas. When the infections specialist came in, he began to take several blood samples as well as perform other tests on LaRicko to try and see what was going on. As the specialist studied my son's condition, his first findings were that it appeared that the staff was giving my son an antibiotic (medication) that was not agreeing with his system, but before the specialist confirmed that statement, he took the blood samples to the lab and said that he would let us know for sure the results later that afternoon.

Well, later on that evening, the doctor returned to confirm that it was the medication that was not agreeing with LaRicko's system; the specialist began to check my son's throat to find that my son's throat was covered with a bad thrush that was caused from the medication that the staff was giving him. That medication also caused LaRicko's elevated temperature as well as high blood pressure. To me, that explained why my son appeared to be so irritated; his throat looked terrible, and to have a tracheotomy in his throat, a feeding tube in his stomach, IVs in his arm, and a cathedra—that was all terrible. I thanked God that it was the medication and not a destroyed splint in LaRicko's brain. And also it was discovered that what the staff were seeing in LaRicko's legs were not blood clots; it was signs of irritation that was caused by the wrong medication (praise the Lord). So the staff began to change his medication immediately, but being that the infection was still in LaRicko's body, we were informed that visitors weren't allowed to come in at that point because I was told that my son was very contagious. Even when my son's fiancée, his dad, and I would go into the room to visit LaRicko, we'd have to wear a gown and a face mask. Was that starting to get crazy or what?

The next day when LaRicko appeared to have calmed down a bit, I was sitting in his room, looking out of the window as I began to pray. I said to the Lord, "Lord, you don't have to prove anything to me. I know you, Lord . . . I trust you, Lord . . . And I've also seen your miracles." I thought about years ago when my youngest brother was very ill, and while he was in intensive care, the doctor had given up on him. The doctor said they'd done all they could do for my brother, and if my brother would make it, it would only be by the grace of God. I remember during that crisis when I was so worried about my brother, and I'd go in and out of the chapel at the hospital and pray for him. I'd also watch my mother and father through that whole time. I remembered that it was around Thanksgiving, and my mother was standing in the kitchen preparing a Thanksgiving dinner as my father and I were getting ready to go to the hospital, which was two hours away. As I stood in the kitchen, I asked my mother, "Are you not going to the hospital?" And she responded, "No, I'll have dinner ready when you all get back," and I was in such disbelief. I said, "Mother, how can you be so calm and be able to prepare a dinner in such a crisis as this one?" I'll never forget when she looked up at me, she said, "I've prayed and I've put it in God's hand, and I've left it there." At that point, I'd heard of that phrase before (putting a situation in the Lord's hand, and leaving it there), but obviously, I didn't have the complete understanding of doing something such as that. So Dad and I left and headed to the hospital to see my brother, and ever so often as we traveled down the highway, I pondered about what my mother had said because I knew she had to know what she was talking about. But as we were growing up, this same brother would get very ill all the time, and the doctors had already told my parents that my brother wasn't going to live past six years old, and at that point, he was twenty plus years old, so with praying parents, I saw what God could do. And now with my parents' prayers, that same brother is a walking miracle, who was by my side and had been praying with me that whole time of LaRicko's illness. Horace is doing awesome. I'm always encouraged by my parents. When my younger brother was born to my parents, my mother had such a hard time with her pregnancy. When she went in the delivery room, the doctors had to perform a C-section on her; there were so many complications going on at the time that my mother hemorrhaged and died on the operating table. The surgeon, who was a Christian man, refused to believe that she was dead; he asked the staff to place her in a private room where he stayed and prayed for her from 7:30 p.m. that day until 2:00 a.m. The doctor sat *down at her bedside where she was lying with his head bowed, praying over my mother's body with tears flowing down his face. After a while, he looked up and noticed that she was awake, and she asked, "Where am I?" He raised his head up even farther and asked, "Honey, how do you feel? Are you hurting?" And he called to the staff to come and see that my mother was still very much alive. He said, "I knew that God did not take her!" And now I can truly say I've seen miracles in my life; my mother who was pronounced dead is truly alive and spreading the Word of God to this day. She is an Evangelist and a missionary in her church where she has served for years. God has a plan and purpose over each and every one of our lives. So as I thought about all those things, sitting there staring out of the window, I began to tell the Lord, "Lord, I believe every word that I've read in the Bible. I believe that Moses stretched out his rod and split the Red Sea, and the people walked across on dry land, which is found in the book of **Hebrews 11:29***

[By Faith they passed through the Red sea as by dry land: which the Egyptians assaying to do were drowned].*"*

*I continued with "I believe that you turned water into wine. I believe Lazarus was raised from the dead, which is found in the book of **John 11:43-44***

[And when he thus had spoken, he cried with a loud voice, Lazarus, come forth. And he that was dead came forth, bound hand and foot with graveclothes: and his face was bound about with a napkin. Jesus saith unto them, loose him, and let him go].*"*

I continued with "Lord, you know, you don't have to prove anything to me." I asked the Lord to please just show the people around me that were saying that LaRicko was completely brain-dead and that my son would never be anything but a vegetable; show them that you are still in the miracle-working business. And I prayed, "Weeping may endure for a night, but joy cometh in the morning, as found in the book of **Psalm 30:5**

[For his anger endureth but a moment; in his favour is life: weeping may endure for a night, but joy cometh in the morning].*"*

But I continued with "Lord, how long is my night?"

Chapter 4

Fighting to Survive

As I sat there in the chair in LaRicko's hospital room staring out the window at the raindrops and praying, I decided to look around at my son to find that he was actually trying to sit up in bed. I stood on my feet and walked over to him, and I said to LaRicko, "Baby, if you want to sit up, blink for me," and I looked him in the face, and he blinked. I was a bit nervous being that he had all the tubes in his body. I said to LaRicko, "I'm going to place my hands behind your back and count to three, and we'll try to sit you up, okay?" And he blinked as if to say he was agreeing with me. Well, when I counted "One . . . two . . . three," I helped my son to rise up almost to a sitting position. As I was doing that, a nurse entered LaRicko's room, and to her surprise, she saw me holding him up. She said, "Great, let me *help you." So I laid my son back down so that we could get a better grip on him. The nurse walked to the opposite side of LaRicko, and I was on the other side, and we placed our hands behind his back, and we lifted him up at the same time, and he appeared to have looked at the nurse and back at me, and he burst out with a laugh (praise God).*

Praise ye the Lord. Praise God in his sanctuary: praise him in the firmament of his power. (Psalm 150:1)

Needless to say, that was a great day for me.

Well, the next day, I prayed that when I walked into my son's room, things were going to continue to look positive; but needless to say, when I got there, he was lying there, not only looking as if he was staring into space, but his IV needle had came out of his arm and blood was all over his gown. I called for a nurse, and when she came in, right away the nurse said, "That IV keeps coming out of his arm," and I asked her, "What do you mean?" And she informed me that the same thing had happened earlier in the day prior to me getting to the hospital, and she didn't know what was going on with that situation, but she said they were short of staff that day, so she didn't know how long he had been bleeding each time before someone showed up to take care of LaRicko. Just when I thought things were looking positive, here we were fighting again to keep him alive; of course it's obvious that the staff felt that my son was a dead man, so it was a proven factor to me that nobody cared. As that day went on, LaRicko's condition began to really appear to be going in reverse. I decided to stay the night with him since he was having such a rough time. And throughout the whole night, he did not go to sleep. His vital signs were out of control because he just could not relax. The nurse had even given him medication to relax him, but his body appeared to be fighting against that. I prayed all night long for my son to go to sleep, but needless to say, he didn't.

The next day was the twenty-third of August, which was the original date that was set for my son and his fiancée to get married. I was so disappointed because I just knew he'd be better by now, but LaRicko was still lying there in a deep coma. His nurse came into the room to clean him up, and as she was doing that, she accidentally broke a piece of the ventilator off, which was keeping his breathing regulated. It appeared that that nurse didn't know what she was doing because it took her so long to get things done, and then she realized after a while that she needed some help to get my son's breathing back on track with the ventilator. I began to pray.

In God have I put my trust: I will not be afraid what man can do to me. (Psalm 56:11)

As I watched LaRicko, I noticed that his face was twitching. So when his technician for the evening came in the room that day, I asked her what did she think was going on with my son's face, and she said what appeared to be happening was LaRicko's brain was trying to reset itself, and with that in mind, my spirits were lifted because to me, at that moment, my prayers were being answered one step at a time.

Well, the next morning, the doctor ordered for LaRicko's ventilator tubes to be cleaned, and as the nurse tried to clean it up, there things went again. The tubes just kept popping off the breathing machine. The nurses just kept having one issue after another. I'm still praying and asking the Lord, "Am I doing the right thing to hold on to my son?" Because I don't *want him to stay here and continue to suffer because things just kept on getting worse and worse with my baby. It was getting so hard for me to watch my son as he continued to lose weight, and his hands continued to retract under at the wrist. It was getting harder and harder to watch this happen to LaRicko. And just to remind you, those things are happening because the staff did not perform physical therapy on my son because we had been told there was no need to perform physical therapy being that my son was completely brain-dead, so the staff wouldn't try to help us in that area. One of the physical therapists informed me that being that LaRicko was in a coma; it was pretty difficult to perform physical therapy on him.*

As we went on with our crisis, a neighbor of mine came out to the hospital to see my son, and she was a neighbor who actually watched LaRicko grow up from a little boy to the young man that he was. My neighbor told me later on that day after she had seen LaRicko that she'd begun to ask people to pray for me because she knew it was going to be so hard on me when I lose my son. She included that once she looked at LaRicko that day at the hospital, there was no way he was going to live through that. And then as that day went on after that negative thought, one of my closest friends came to visit us at the hospital as well, and I was very disappointed in my friend because he wanted me to leave the hospital and go home to locate the life insurance policy for LaRicko, which made me feel that he didn't think my son was going to live either. Those were the kinds of comments that kept my spirits so low. And surely I didn't need that. But I knew that I had to continue to pray harder to get past all that negativity.

I'll never forget while sitting in church service one Sunday morning, my pastor was preaching on how we sometimes need to clean house.

He didn't mean as in dusting the furniture or vacuuming the floors and so on and so forth as in housework. Pastor said to me, "Diane, you are waiting on the Lord to bless you and LaRicko, but you've got people around you that are coming to your house [hospital] that's not with you." My pastor included, "When you leave church today, you need to go and clean house. Everyone that's showing up is not praying the same prayer you are. There's people in your house that's just coming and can't wait to see you fall, and some of the people are just spectators just coming to see what's going on." As my pastor continued with his sermon, I pondered on what Pastor had said. While sitting there in the church services, I cried uncontrollably. After service was over that day, I could hardly wait to leave church so that I could go home because I had some housecleaning to get done. When I got to the hospital that afternoon, I began to request the nurses to make sure that there weren't any visitors coming in to see my son if I wasn't there at the hospital. That idea for whatever reasons felt so good, it appeared to have been the thing to have done. I only wanted my pastor and other ministers to come into my son's room, and other that, only the doctors and the nurses should have been in LaRicko's room. Day after day as the time went on, you could really see that my son was not being cared for properly. I noticed how irritated he was looking around the neck area where the tube was in his throat. Even the tube in his stomach had begun to be a bit irritated.

I didn't know what to do other than continue to pray.

And all things, whatsoever ye shall ask in prayer, believing, ye shall receive. (Matthew 21:22)

There seemed to have been only one nurse who was working at that hospital who'd really take care of my son, and he wasn't due in until that

Friday night, and it was only Tuesday. Lord, my heart was so heavy. I'm just watching my son get worse and worse.

That afternoon while I was at work, I received the most unexpected phone call from one of the caseworkers of the hospital who had examined my son's case at that hospital during his stay. I really didn't know what to say at that time. That caseworker called and asked me what was I going to do with my son because the hospital couldn't continue to keep LaRicko there. The caseworker continued with "You need to get him out of here." That caseworker spoke about my son as if he was not human. The caseworker said, "If you're not going to have your son checked into a nursing home where he would expire nor unplug him, then you can just come to the hospital and pack LaRicko's bags and take him home with you today." While holding the phone in complete numbness all over my body, After a few moments of silence to collect what I was hearing, my only response was okay because I had no idea of what I was going to be doing with my son. The Lord knew that I didn't want my son in a nursing home. I wanted my son to be released to a rehabilitation center where he would have been receiving physical therapy at some point, but of course, the doctor did not see things the way I did because the staff were trying to get me to understand that LaRicko was completely brain-dead, and he couldn't be rehabbed. The caseworker also said in the phone conversation that LaRicko was never going to be anything but a vegetable, so I was wasting time trying to keep him alive. But at the same time, as I thought about taking LaRicko home with tubes all in his body, I knew that there was no way I could take care of him properly. And as I was standing up at the front area of the office after I had hung up the phone from speaking to the caseworker, I began to talk with my manager regarding the conversation that I just had with that caseworker, sharing with the manager what I was told. There was another employee that was standing there listening to the conversation also regarding the disturbing news that I had just received regarding taking my son home. And when I finished sharing how disappointed I was about that to my manager, the employee that was standing there listening to the conversation said to me, "Lois, the lottery is 220 million dollars. You should just buy a ticket and try and win the lottery, and then you can just unplug LaRicko and buy you another son." I really couldn't believe what my ears were hearing, but I had to quickly remind myself that the world was made up of all kinds of people. I said, "Lord, forgive him, for he knew not what he was saying!"

I started to pray to the Lord that people were beginning to look at me as if I were crazy, but I had even begun to tell people that I am crazy enough to believe that the Lord was going to heal my son. I had gone a step further to say LaRicko was going to be fine; he's going to walk down those halls at that hospital and show the people that God is yet in the miracle-working business. I would say that to the people as if I knew, without a doubt in my mind, what I was talking about. But when I would look back at my son, I didn't see any of that happening with my natural eyes. But I knew in my heart that I had the faith, and I knew that without faith, it was impossible to please God.

And Jesus said unto them, Because of your unbelief: for verily I say unto you, If ye have faith as a grain of mustard seed, ye shall say unto this mountain, Remove hence to yonder place; and it shall remove; and nothing shall be impossible unto you. (Matthew 17:20)

So I would say, "Lord, it's up to you now."

I've expressed how much I trust the Lord in my heart, and I knew that even if the Lord didn't bring LaRicko out of that situation, I knew with all my heart that God can do it. Well, after I began searching for a rehabilitation center here in the city limits, I was not fortunate. Of course, none of the facilities would accept my son because of the condition that he was in. The caseworker had told me that being that LaRicko was in a comatose condition, there was no way a rehabilitation facility would ever consider accepting him. And I had really began to get even more disappointed than I was in the beginning because I did not want to place my son in a nursing home. I just knew that if I would have placed him in a nursing home, it would have really been the end of my son's life. But the nursing home appeared to have been the only opportunity I had at that time being that my son was in a coma and he had a tracheotomy, so the doctor had begun to give me several names of different nursing homes. So I began to place phone calls to several of those nursing homes to inquire about the qualifications for my son being place in their facilities to find that they would not accept him because he had a tracheotomy. The issue with a tracheotomy had begun to be the disqualifying factor for LaRicko. Then I had begun to place phone calls to several rehab centers in the area to find that I really didn't stand a chance with any of them either. And these issues continued mainly because LaRicko was in a comatose condition as well as the tubes all over him. Later on that day, one of the social workers called to inform me that the only rehabilitation that would probably consider accepting my son was four hours away from St. Louis, and I almost hit the floor. The last thing I wanted to think of was having LaRicko four hours away from me in that condition. I felt that my son needed his mother (me) close to him, being that he was in a coma. He needs me through this process more than ever, I thought to myself. I really was almost sick about the sound of that option.

My brother Horace called to check on me (he was always on the phone or in St. Louis checking on LaRicko and me), and when he called a few minutes after the disturbing phone call that I had received regarding my son's only option of being relocated four hours away, I began to share with Horace the issue that I was up against. I was so confused and upset, and as usual, Horace always had words of comfort for me. Horace informed me that he'd spoken with someone at a Memphis rehabilitation center regarding LaRicko being transferred to their facility because my brother wanted to try and relieve some of the pressure off me. I thought that was very generous of him to have considered doing that for me, but I also fought with that thought in my mind because I felt that I'm totally responsible for taking care of my son. And I didn't want to place my responsibilities on anyone else. So then I struggled with whether I should go with the Memphis idea or release LaRicko to Mount Vernon. Either way, I'd be four hours away from my son. The decisions were beginning to get more difficult for me as time went on. Well, the big debate was on between my brother and me because my brother wanted to be supportive by transferring LaRicko to Memphis.

So I called the Memphis facilities and spoke with someone regarding my son being transferred there, and of course they were very nice and supportive with all the information that I needed, and the nurse asked me to let them know when I wanted to transfer my son to their facility. And it was very helpful because Horace had already gone by the rehabilitation center in Memphis prior to me contacting them and spoke with someone regarding the idea of my son transferring there, which made it easier for me. But believe it or not, I couldn't relax with that decision. So I continued to pray that the Lord would direct me to the best facility for my son so that I wouldn't have to travel such a far distance to spend time with him. It was already obvious that none of the facilities in the city

*limits would accept him. So after a disturbing day, it was time for me
to head to the hospital to see my son. I remember squeezing my hands
tight together and stomping my feet, saying, "Lord, **you said** in your
Word that you will not leave me nor forsake me. Lord, **you said** that no
weapon formed against me shall be able to prosper." I was getting a
bit frustrated and felt that I needed to remind the Lord of several of the
things that **he said in his Word** because the **Lord's Word** was the **faith**
and **trust** that I was **standing on**.*

*Well, when I entered the hospital, I had begun to do my usual praying
as I was headed down the hall to LaRicko's room. I would pray that my
son would be sitting there on the side of his bed, waiting to say, "Mom,
what took you so long to come and pick me up?" Because I knew that
the god that I served could do all things, and I know that I had the faith.
But needless to say, when I entered my son's room, I couldn't believe my
eyes. His arm was at least three times the normal size. As I stood there
upset, I began to pray. Afterward, I buzzed for a nurse as I've always
had to do when I got to the hospital because the staff was always so busy
with other patients but did not have enough time for my son. When the
nurse entered the room, I began to question her with "Why is my son's
arm looking like this? What is going on? I asked. And of course, the
nurse replied that she didn't understand how that could have happened
to him being that the IV that was placed in LaRicko's arm was not in a
vein; it was just flowing through his arm, and my son's arm was literally
looking and moving as if it was a water balloon. As I continued to watch
the staff there at the hospital, they began to constantly drop the ball
when it came to caring for LaRicko. I had begun to wonder if it was just
time for me to end his suffering. But every time that would come to my
mind, I would remind myself that my son knew that if anybody would
fight for his life, it would definitely be his mother (me), so I couldn't give*

up at that point. I just needed to continue to pray for guidance from the Lord and be patient.

Plead my cause, O Lord, with them that strive with me: fight against them that fight against me. Take hold of shield and buckler, and stand up for mine help. (Psalm 35:1-2)

I continued to make phone calls one after another to try and keep my son here in the city limits with me, but I had no such luck in that area. I called my son's aunt to ask her if she could sit with LaRicko one weekend while I make a surprise visit to the facility that I was suggested to check out. Of course his aunt replied yes, but she also wanted to know why the doctor wanted to send him so far away. I began to explain to her that none of the rehabilitation centers or nursing homes in the city limits would accept LaRicko because of the condition that he was in. So his aunt was very disappointed about that as well. So LaRicko's aunt contacted someone she knew with prayers that this individual could help us in that area of keeping LaRicko here in the city limits. I was very anxious about that because now I felt that my son was going to be able to stay in the city limits, and I could continue to visit with him every day.

Well, as I spoke with that person regarding the issue that I was facing, that individual informed me of all the things that I needed to have done in order to make that happen. And right away I began to take care of all those things. Finally, I was at least feeling better with the thought that my son would be here in the city limits through the rest of his recovery. And that entire time, I continued to pray, "Lord, give me the best recovery facility for my son." I can hardly wait for LaRicko to get better.

Chapter 5

Recognizing God's Presence

Here I was again with another Friday night of praying that my son does not have another rough night. I spent the night with him again, and I was sitting on the side of the bed talking to him as I always did, and his eyes were focused straight ahead. I would continue to wave my hands in front of his eyes just to see if he'd ever blink, and of course he didn't, but that didn't stop me from standing strong on my faith. After I talked to my son for a while, I continued to look out the window. I decided after about a half an hour to prepare myself to lie down for the evening. One of the nurses who were nice to us at the beginning of our visit brought in a roll-away bed so that whoever spent the night with LaRicko would at least have a bed to lie down on. So I began to let my bed down for the evening when one young lady came in and informed me the name of my son's nurse for the evening. I was a bit disappointed because here we go again with a new name that after about a month there, I hadn't heard of that nurse. I would always pray for a nurse that was at least familiar with what was going on with my son; even though it didn't appear that things were being done properly, but at least they were familiar with LaRicko's condition.

So when I began to express my feelings to that young lady, she said to me that the nurse was really a nice lady, very quiet and very religious. Hum . . . Is she really?" I asked. The young lady looked at the expression on my face and knew I was okay with the fact that the nurse was very religious. So as I began to relax on the bed, I waited on the nurse to show up in my son's room, and it took most of the night before she showed up in LaRicko's room. Go figure! So while the night was very quiet and my son appeared to be at last resting, he wasn't asleep. But he was quiet and appeared to be relaxed.

Just when I thought we could just relax the rest of the evening, one of the CNAs' came in and said it was time for her to change the linen on LaRicko's bed, so I began to sat up while she was changing the linen on the bed, and she talked to me a little bit, but what I most remembered about her was she would sing the whole time she was working, and the song that she was singing happened to be one of my favorite songs. The song was **"I Won't Complain."** And that CNA was just singing that song as Mahalia Jackson would have. It was as if I was at a church service. I have always loved when my pastor would sing that song because it would always touch my spirit. So as she continued to sing, I began to pray for peace of mind, and I would ask the Lord to continue to order my next steps. **(Precious Lord, take my hand and lead me on.)**

When the CNA finished changing the linens on LaRicko's bed, the nurse for the night finally showed up. She came in, and she was very quiet. I spoke to her when she came into my son's room, and she spoke very lightly. And she began to take LaRicko's blood pressure and his other vital signs, and she asked, "Is that your son?" I said, "Yes, it is." She asked, "What happened?" And I began to tell her, and she continued with "Well, you need to talk to him," and I responded with "Yes, I do that continually." And she also included, "You need to tell him where he is. Tell him he is in the hospital and let him know what happened and let him know you are praying for him." Well, as the nurse was saying that, I watched my son as his eyes began to look up over his head as if he was watching that nurse as she was talking and taking his vital signs, and when she said "tell him that he is in the hospital and that you are praying for him," he began to cry. I looked at him because I knew how much he feared hospitals. I tried to calm him down by pampering him and saying, "Baby, I'm here with you, and you are okay." So I began to get a little upset inside because that nurse was upsetting my son by making those statements in front of him. I was asking myself, Why didn't the nurse take me outside the door to suggest those things to me? I didn't want anything else to be stressing LaRicko even though he was in a coma. So every time that nurse came into LaRicko's room, I was praying that she wouldn't say anything else to upset my son, and I noticed that every time that nurse would walk into the room, she would never turn on the bright lights, and LaRicko's eyes would appear to be following her everywhere she went. These reactions were really a big difference for LaRicko. My son had never appeared to be that alert until that point. I was so caught up in being upset because my son was crying that I hadn't even realized that he was showing signs of emotion as well as realizing that a brain-dead person can't possibly show any signs of emotion. God had showed up that night and I was missing it. Whether we realize it or not, there's so many times that God shows up in our lives, and we're so caught in expecting things to appear different that we miss our blessings.

And when the dew that lay was gone up, behold, upon the face of the wilderness there lay a small round thing, as small as the hoar frost on the ground. And when the children of Israel saw it, they said one to another, It is manna: for they wist not what it was. And Moses said unto them, This is the bread which the Lord hath given you to eat. (Exodus 16:14-15)

I lay back down and begun to rub my son's hand to calm him down, and I kept saying to him, "You're okay, Momma's here," and that seemed to have calmed him down each time. After a while, we both fell off to sleep.

Early that next morning, I was sitting at LaRicko's bedside watching him to notice if I was going to see any kind of reactions from him, his face, his body movement, or just something positive. But my son remained pretty quiet. I got up and began to wash his face and brush his teeth. And while I was combing LaRicko's hair, I had begun to share with him what the doctor had suggested regarding him transferring to another facility. I explained to him that I was going to take a drive up to visit the one facility that was four hours away from us, but I was going to make sure that I felt good about it prior to transferring him there. As I continued to comb my son's hair, I asked him if he wanted to get better to blink one time for me . . . And he did. So I continued to explain to him that the place would help him to get better because it was a rehabilitation center. Afterward, his face started to look so sad as if he was going to cry, so I told him not to worry. I assured him that I was going to be with him no matter where they had to take him. I told my son that I just wanted the best for him during his recovery because the staff was not doing what it takes for him there at the hospital. After a while, as I was standing there combing LaRicko's hair, I felt that he must have been okay with the idea because he fell asleep.

I called my son's aunt to see if she could come over and sit with LaRicko for that day while I went home and made preparations to take care of some needed documents, which could have possibly kept my son in a rehabilitation center within the city limits. And I had also decided to take advantage of the rest of that day by taking the drive to the rehabilitation center that was four hours away so that I would at least become familiar with the facility as well as the drive there.

So I called my best friend and shared with her what I was up against regarding LaRicko needing to be moved from that hospital real soon, and I informed her that I was not sure about the facility that was suggested to me because it was so far away from us, being that I wanted to be with LaRicko every day. And I continued to explain to my best friend that I could have probably kept LaRicko in the city limits if I could have gotten certain documents in place by that Monday morning.

So right away, my best friend, being the wonderful person that she is, said we were going to take a drive that day right after I got the documents that I needed put in place. So as soon as we could, we got all the documents together and had the paperwork typed up right away and got the documents notarized a couple of hours later. Once we took care of that, we got ready and made a four-hour drive to the rehabilitation center that was suggested to me.

On the way to the facility, I began to pray and ask the Lord that if that was the best place for my son, for the Lord to guide me and help me to recognize what he has for us. As we drove hours down the highway, I kept thinking to myself that the facility was too far for my baby to be from me. I could not come to terms with that being the place for him because I felt that he needed to be closer to me. But I figured that being that we were already on our way there; it was no reason for me not to at least check the place out. My best friend knew a guy, Jesse, that was very familiar with that facility, and as we were riding down the highway, she decided to call Jesse to ask him questions regarding the rehab center. And Jesse had begun to tell my friend how excellent the place was. He told her that his dad had been placed in that center and that his dad was doing great. Jesse even included that if they hadn't transferred his dad hours away from the city, his mother would have tired herself too much by running back and forth to the hospital every day. And Jesse said that his mother didn't even realize that it was not good for her health. So Jesse included that he felt that this would be a good move for me because I needed time to relax, and it was going to be best for me to visit with my son on the weekends. And at that point, I had begun to feel better for a minute after he said that. So I pondered about that for a few minutes, and actually my first thought was, Jesse has got to be crazy, because my son didn't need to be that far from me. And then on second thought, maybe that was going to be best for both of us. But of course, I was still praying and asking the Lord to order my steps on that decision. So as we continued to drive down the highway, we discussed the thought of me transferring LaRicko, and my best friend said to me that I really needed to start getting some rest as well. But I reminded her that being that my son was in the condition that he was in, I couldn't get any rest with LaRicko being that far away from me. But my friend said that being that we were doing that surprise visit to the

*facility that I would get my feel from that and make my decision after
that, and I agreed with her.*

*After four hours of driving and talking, I did realize that it really
wasn't a bad trip, and when we drove up to the center, I began to look
around and noticed that the facility was an extremely nice area from the
outside; it was also in such a secluded and quiet part of the town. The
area was very impressive starting from the outer appearance.*

*Well, after my best friend parked the car, we got out and began to
walk toward the front door of the facility. And as were walking, we also
were admiring everything around the area. When we made it to the front
door and went inside, there sat the receptionist at the front desk. Okay,
I said to myself, here goes the test. We spoke to the receptionist, and she
spoke back to us, and she appeared to be very nice. So I had begun to
explain to her the reason for my visit. I asked her if I could possibly have
the opportunity to tour the facility, being that I was considering having
my son transferred there. The receptionist responded, "Of course you
can." She picked up the phone and called up the head nurse that was
there for the weekend, and the receptionist told me that the nurse was
on her way down to get me so that she could take me on a tour of their
facility. Wow! I thought to myself that being that we didn't call and give
them an advance notice that we were coming, I didn't think that the
welcome would have been so receptive. But I was so wrong!*

*After I waited for a few minutes, the head nurse came down to the
main floor, greeted us, and then she introduced herself. She was so nice
to us also. As the head nurse began to walk us through the facility, she
explained each area thoroughly, from beginning to end. She pointed out
the intensive care area as well as the trauma center. She explained to*

me the different programs that each patient would be going through and included that the facility was the second-best rehabilitation center in the nation. I was really impressed with the visit. She also informed me that the facility also had accommodations for the families to come and stay while visiting with their loved ones. That was really awesome! I thought, We'd be right on the premises with my son if I should bring him here. And the best was yet to come. The nurse said to me that 98 percent of their patients walked out of their facility. Well, of course that was what I wanted to hear. I prayed and said to the Lord I claimed the 98 percent chance that my son was going to walk out of there. So once the tour was over, the nurse walked us back to the front door where I thanked her so much for taking the time to do that for me. And I included, "I will see you soon!" And the nurse said that she was looking forward to having my son transferred there.

As we left the center, I had begun to ask my best friend what were her thoughts of the facility and the tour. She replied that she thought that it was very nice. And she reminded me of what the head nurse had said regarding that 98 percent of their patients walked out; that sounded great to me.

On the drive back home, I felt pretty excited on one hand. But of course, on the other hand, I was still stuck on the distance that was going to be between me and my son. As we continued our drive back, I called LaRicko's aunt, who was sitting with him while we took the trip, to check on my son at the hospital to see how his day went, and she informed me that he had a very nice and quiet day with her. I was glad to hear that he had done well that day because for some reason, the past couple of days he had been having ongoing issues with his bowel movements. So anyway, I began to tell his aunt about the nice facility and asked her to pray with me on the right move to make for LaRicko. And afterward, we continued on our very nice drive back to St. Louis. The weather was beautiful, and everything just went so well on the drive going to the facility and coming back home. Thank you, Lord.

When we made it back in town, I checked to see if I needed to go back to the hospital to spend time with LaRicko, but his fiancée had already made it back for the evening. His fiancée was so supportive; she was there every night so that I could stay home and prepare for work the next morning. His fiancée said that LaRicko appeared to be pretty relaxed. So I decided to go home and wait until the next day to go to the hospital and visit with LaRicko. After I got home, I continued to pray about the situation regarding transferring my son because I wanted to make sure that I made the right decision.

The next morning when I got out of bed, I had begun to prepare myself for church. While I was there at church, I began to pray so hard for answers. I didn't know which way to go with things, but I was praying. "Lord, please give me the knowledge to know when you are speaking to me. Lord, help me to make the right decision on the facility that was best for LaRicko," I prayed. So many people at the church were praying with me on my decision as well as for my son's healing. I thanked God for my church family. My church was where I was being molded into the Christian that I was praying to become. And that had been one of my greatest challenges, to trust God as well continuing to stand strong on my faith.

Jesus answered and said unto them, Verily I say unto you, If ye have faith, and doubt not, ye shall not only do this which is done to the fig tree, but also if ye shall say

unto this mountain, Be thou removed, and be thou cast into the sea; it shall be done. (Matthew 21:21)

After leaving church services that day, I headed for the hospital to visit my son. I was anxious to spend some time with him being that I was gone most of the day before traveling to the facility. When I got to the hospital, I walked into LaRicko's room, kissed him, and I began to tell him about the services we had at church. And I'd always repeat the twenty-third psalm to him. So as I began to comb his hair, I kissed him again and began to repeat the twenty-third psalm, and after that, I told my son how much I loved him. Shortly after I was there, the nurse entered the room, and I asked her how were things going with him, and she informed me that my son still hadn't had a bowel movement, which had gone on for more than a couple of days, and they were really concerned about that issue because they just couldn't figure out what was actually going on. So there we were again, with one issue after another. With so many issues constantly occurring one after another, that was why I felt my son needed to remain close to me. Not that I felt I could stop those issues from occurring, but at least I could be there in case we would have been dealing with more inconsiderate people. My son just seemed to have gone through enough hard times.

As time was passing on, I still had concerns on my mind, but I was just going through the motions, not really feeling anything, because it was so much for me to decide. But early that next morning, about 2:00 a.m., my son finally had a bowel movement, and believe it or not, we were so happy. But the doctor still could not at that time figure out what was going on with LaRicko's system to have continued to go through that issue. And later in the morning when the doctor came in to check on LaRicko, he noticed again that he was not being cared for in the area of his tracheotomy. The doctor said to me that there was an unusual *color in my son's trachea. As I had said before, my son's condition was starting to feel as if it were a roller coaster. His condition had been a constant up-and-down upsetting battle.*

The nurse and the tech had come in for the evening to check on LaRicko, and those two people were very supportive of my son. I was always so happy when they'd come to care for him, but once they looked my son over, they were very honest with me regarding his condition. The nurse told me that things with my son were not looking good at all. That particular nurse included how it was obvious that the other nurses were not doing the things that they were supposed to be doing to care for my son. My son's tube in his stomach was starting to show an ugly color as well as the tracheotomy in his neck. The nurse told me that LaRicko was beginning to get an infection, which did not sound good at all.

All of a sudden, my son began to get restless. He was appearing to have pain in his left arm again. He'd frown up as if he was in severe pain as well pulling his left arm up toward his body as if he was experiencing excruciating pain. So I felt that something should have been done about that. With me constantly complaining about the issue that my son was in pain, the doctor said to me again that those were only reflexes from my son's body because he couldn't possibly have known that he was in pain. I was reminded once again that LaRicko's brain was dead. But in order to make me feel better, the doctor ordered some muscle relaxers for LaRicko.

My mother and my brother, Horace, came up to visit with us on that weekend. I was so happy to see them. My mother and I sat with LaRicko most of that day so that she could monitor his reactions. For some reason, my son was very quiet. My mother's profession was a nurse as well, and she was just outdone with what was really going on with LaRicko.

When she first came up to visit us when the issue first happened, at least my son looked like himself, but weeks later when Mom and my brother came up to visit, my son had become skin and bones, and his hands were completely retracted under. He had just begun to look as if he was retarded. Mom never said it to me, but I almost felt that she wanted me to just give up because it had been such a long time, and LaRicko's diagnosis hadn't changed. So as that day went on, my brother spent the night with LaRicko and wanted me to stay away from the hospital so that I could get some rest, and he didn't want me to call back that night at all. He felt that I needed a break from it all. I loved him for that, and I knew it was going to be hard for me to do that. But I said okay.

Well, as that evening came, Horace said to my mother, "Take Diane shopping or something, and get her out of here so that me and LaRicko can spend some time together." He is always so comical and such a family-oriented brother that I knew that LaRicko was in good hands with my brother around. So my mother and I left the hospital and went shopping, and I could not stay off the phone checking on my son, and I thought my brother was so funny because when I called and my brother answered the phone, he said to me LaRicko said to tell me to stop calling there. My brother, Horace, always would try lifting my spirits. And when my brother was in Memphis, he would call me every day and all throughout the day to keep my spirits lifted. So that was great, but I still could not relax my mind. But my mother and I continued to spend some quality time together shopping, and we also went out to a restaurant and ate. Then we came back to the house where several of my family members came over to visit with us.

On that next morning when I got back to the hospital, I walked into my son's room where my brother was relaxing with him; everything appeared to be okay. My brother had bought LaRicko an inspirational bracelet to place on LaRicko's wrist in July when he first went into a coma, and when my brother returned for that second visit, he bought himself the same bracelet and exchanged bracelets with LaRicko, and the bracelet read, **FEAR NOT.**

Yea, though I walk through the valley of the shadow of death, I will fear no evil: for thou art with me; thy rod and thy staff they comfort me. (Psalm 23:4)

I thought that was a very nice thing to have done. Horace said that he had talked to LaRicko throughout the night and he prayed with my son as well. I was very happy to hear that. And as the day went on, Mom and Horace had to head home. I really hated to see them go, but I was so appreciative that they came to St. Louis to check on us.

As they were leaving the hospital, I walked them out to the parking lot where I hugged them and said good-bye. Afterward, I turned around and began to walk down the hall back to my son's room when, to my surprise, I saw a guy who worked for the hospital's housekeeping department. I hadn't seen that guy since my son was in the intensive care unit on another floor. I was sitting there in the waiting area when that guy walked up and began to talk to me. And he was surprised that the young man that was in the intensive care unit that was pronounced to be completely brain-dead was my son. He said to me that he could tell that I must have the Lord on my side because I was walking around, encouraging and smiling with other people there at the hospital, when I had a crisis of my own. He offered me a soda or coffee, which I thought was very nice of him. And when my son was moved from the intensive care area, which was on another floor, he thought we had left the hospital all together because he hadn't seen us anymore. When the guy saw me walking down the hall, he was so happy because he said he had wondered about us. That guy would always be waxing the floors; he kept the halls shining. He began to ask me about my son, and I told him that LaRicko was right down the hall; and I included that the diagnosis was still the same, but I shared with him about my faith in God.

He said to me that he could tell that I was standing on faith. I enjoyed our conversation because we talked about the Bible the whole time, and he encouraged me so much because he talked about faith being the substance of things hoped for and the evidence of things not seen, which is found in the book of **Hebrews 11:1.** *He and I talked for a long time down the hallway from my son's room. I said to the guy that my son was going to be a miracle and he was going to walk down those nicely waxed floors, and that guy agreed with me, but he reminded me that if I was speaking from faith, then I needed to stop saying that my son was going to be a testimony. He reminded that I should be saying, "My son is a testimony." He said to me, "In case you don't realize it, when your son made it out of the intensive care unit, he was already a testimony." That was interesting to me because I hadn't thought of it in that way. It is something how people come into our lives for one reason or another. And I thought it was great how I had met that guy on the intensive care unit floor, and he said that he had never before that time worked on a Sunday, nor had he ever worked on that floor that my son was on before that time. But he had been asked to work that Sunday and he decided to do it, and that's when he ran into us again, which he counted as a blessing. I had even shared with him that I was going to be transferring my son to the facility that was four hours away from the city limits because the doctor had suggested that it was the best place for him being that my son was in a vegetative state. And I continued with*

I didn't want to have to travel so far to see LaRicko, but I didn't have much of an option. And that guy told me that if transportation was ever an issue for me to just call and let him know. He promised to drive me there every weekend if I needed him to do so. And I thought that was so nice of Mr. Doss, being that he didn't really know us, but his kindness was going to support us as long as we needed him to. That's why I say again, people are brought into our lives for reasons. He appeared to have been such a great blessing.

After our long conversation and praising God for his miracle, I thanked Mr. Doss for touching and agreeing with me on my son's healing. And as I began to walk away, I told Mr. Doss to have a blessed evening, and he said the same. I went into my son's room, and I felt great! I walked over to LaRicko and leaned over and kissed him and began to share the conversation with him that Mr. Doss and I had. I picked up a comb and began to comb my son's hair and told him, "Baby, you know what, you are a miracle, and you are going to walk down these halls and shock those nurses." I told him that Mr. Doss said that he was going to keep those floors waxed and shining because he could hardly wait to see him walk down those halls. I also told him how we were going to come back and shock the people at that hospital because my son was going to walk back into that hospital. My son was just lying there with his eyes open, listening to his mother (me) brag about him. I sat with him and prayed until his fiancée came to the hospital for the evening. Once she got there, we began to discuss the facility that was four hours away because I wanted to know what her thoughts were regarding that, and his fiancée really just wanted to take LaRicko home with her because she felt that she could take care of him herself, being that her profession was already in the hospital/nursing home field. But I didn't feel comfortable with that idea because she was pregnant with their first child, who was my first grandchild, and I didn't want anything to go wrong in that area. I knew after a while that LaRicko's fiancée would not have been able to care for him in her condition. So after she and I continued to discuss those things further in details, she appeared to be okay with my son going to the new facility so that he could begin his recovery. I was so happy to have such a positive person at that time in our lives because his fiancée always felt that LaRicko was going to be fine. She kept saying that she couldn't wait until he got better so that they could go back home to Tennessee. I turned and hugged her as I began to head home to relax for the evening.

The next day, after I arrived at the hospital, I walked into my son's room, and what did I find? My son's ventilator hose had been detached from the ventilator for over twenty minutes. That was the oxygen that was keeping my son's breathing flowing normally. It was getting more difficult each day for me to continue to tolerate those issues. There again I knew that as long as no one was there with my son, none of the nurses would come to care for him properly. I had begun to go to the hospital at all different times just to see what conditions that I would find my son in, and believe me, I was not happy. Thank God that he was always there for us. I had spoken with the doctor and informed her that I had gone and visited the facility in Mount Vernon and that I had considered transferring my son there, and she was happy to hear that, and needless to say, I was aware that we had outgrown the hospital anyway because most of the staff had begun to treat my son as if he was a dead man already. So I had begun to look forward to our next step. My brother really didn't want LaRicko to go that far away from St. Louis because it made the trip even farther for him to travel from Memphis. But I had prayed for the best place for LaRicko during his recovery, and Mount Vernon appeared to have been that place.

The doctor that had been supportive of my son and I came into LaRicko's room to see us, and as he examined LaRicko, he was aware that things weren't getting any better for my son as LaRicko still could not have a bowel movement. And the doctor had tried several different solutions on LaRicko regarding his bowel movement, but nothing appeared to be working for my son. So as the doctor sat there at LaRicko's bedside, he had begun to think of names of other facilities that would probably accept and care for LaRicko better that was not so far away from our city limits. The doctor expressed how much he didn't want to continue to watch LaRicko deteriorate either. The doctor appeared to be sad for me because he knew how much I wanted my son to remain in the city limits. But I had begun to accept the fact that we had to at least try and see if there was something better for LaRicko. So I thanked the doctor for everything that he'd done for us, and I shared with him that we'd decided to go with the idea of Mount Vernon, and the doctor was okay with that idea, and he encouraged me to just hang in there and keep thinking positive. And I agreed to do just that, and I thanked the doctor again as he walked out of LaRicko's room.

As the next day went on, my son continued to take a spiral downhill in his condition. Just when I thought things couldn't get any worse, I received a call from the caseworker of the hospital to inform me that the facility four hours away that I prayed long and hard about had called the hospital and said that their facility had denied my son the opportunity to be transferred there, being that LaRicko was in such bad condition. I could hardly believe that after fighting with that decision for so long and I had finally came to terms with the idea of transferring LaRicko there that the facility denied him. When I entered LaRicko's room that afternoon and saw the condition he was in, immediately I became so upset. I was just ready to leave that hospital right at that *moment! My son's legs somehow had gotten caught up in the bed rails, which caused them to be all scarred, and I was so upset because the last thing he needed were sores on his body being that he was lying in a bed at all times. (Bedsores are very hard to cure.) And when I called for the nurse and she entered the room, she was completely surprised with what she saw. "What happened here?" she asked me. I was looking at the nurse with tears in my eyes because once again, no one had been caring for my son as they should have. The nurse began to question different people in order to find out who had removed the massagers off LaRicko's legs. Of course no one knew nor had the doctor ordered anyone on the staff to remove the massagers from LaRicko's legs. At that point, we had to fight to keep the open wounds from getting infected as well as healed, and I knew that was going to be a hard battle to tolerate. Now the Lord was showing me every day that it was time to transfer my son from that hospital. I had begun to wonder after that incident if that was my sign to just let go of my son because I did not want to watch him continue to suffer any further. My son's legs were a terrible sight, and he was yet at a point that he could not have a bowel movement, and he had gotten so thin. I prayed to the Lord to please bestow me a sign, to grant me something to know whether to continue to hold on to my baby or allow him to rest in peace. It must have been time to let go! I thought to myself. I was so upset that I picked up the phone and I called my mother to share with her what had happened to LaRicko's legs, and she couldn't believe what I was telling her. As we continued to talk shortly afterward, she heard a knock at her door, and she asked me to hold the line for a minute as she went to answer the door. Mom answered the door and came back to the phone and said, "Diane, I'll call you back shortly." But before she hung up the phone, the young man at the door said to my mother "I was on my lunch break, and I'd heard about your grandson being sick, and I wanted to come by and check on you." My mother answered with "Yes, he is in a coma." Then the young man asked Mom, "Is that your daughter on the phone?" My mother said yes. So that young man asked my mother to allow him to speak to me, and he got on the phone. He introduced himself as Prophet Michael, and I said my name, and he said, "Diane, what's your son's name?" I told him, and he asked, "Are you in your son's room?" And I answered with yes. He said, "Diane, go over to LaRicko's bed and place your hands on his legs." And I was so amazed because I hadn't told him anything about my son's legs being bruised and scarred up, and my mother didn't have the opportunity to share that with him prior to him speaking with me on the phone either. I stood there looking at my son with tears in my eyes as Prophet Michael asked, "Do you have your hands on LaRicko's legs?" And I answered yes, and he began to pray for the healing of LaRicko's legs. He continued to pray so strongly for us, and after his prayer, he said to me, "Diane, don't worry. LaRicko is going to be just fine." He continued with "LaRicko is going to shock the doctors and the nurses at the hospital. The Lord is going to heal him, and he will walk down those same hospital halls and be a blessing to other people." I had just spoken with that young prophet in the middle of the day when he was normally at work at that time; he just happened to stop by my parents' house during his lunch break because he had heard about my son, and with that in my mind, nothing just happens. The Lord sent me just what I needed, and that was my sign to hold on to my son a while longer. I said to myself again, Weeping may endure for a night, but our joy was coming in the morning. And that's what I held on to.*

For his anger endureth but a moment; in his favour is life: weeping may endure for a night, but joy cometh in the morning. (Psalm 30:5)

After I had spent another confusing day at the job pondering on where I was going to place my son during his recovery, I headed to the hospital to spend time with my son. I was very thankful that Sister Moore and Sister Blackwell from my church, who had come out periodically the earlier part of the days to sit with my son when I had to be at work and his fiancée had to take care of other things. I thanked God for those two people in my life for being supportive of us. So upon my arrival at the hospital, I walked into my son's room to discover that his IV had worked its way out of his arm somehow, and blood was all over his gown again. His arms were so bruised from the nurses taking blood from him to the IV continuing to come out of his arms for whatever reasons, but that was so hard to continue to tolerate. But I was still praying and trusting God through it all. And of course, the nurses would come in and say the same things over and over, that they don't understand how that happened and to tell me that they were just in there a half an hour ago; it was starting to be as if it was a broken record.

After a while, the doctor came in and began to check LaRicko's CPAP, which was being performed to see how his breathing condition was going. The doctor also felt that it would take an awful long time, if ever, that LaRicko would come off the ventilator. My son's breathing was controlled by that machine totally because every time the doctor would try to turn the oxygen level down, it was as if we were losing my son because he could not breath on his own at all. As my brother and I continued the process of trying to find LaRicko a facility in Memphis that would accept him, I really had begun to get very stressed over that issue because the time was running out for us at the hospital. It was as if the caseworker really was going to send LaRicko home with me regardless of his condition. That caseworker just wanted my son out of their hospital. So wherever I decided to take my son, I needed to make sure that the next facility specialized in ventilators being that LaRicko had to depend on that totally. So I continued to pray to God for guidance as well as his assurance to know whether it was the Lord who was ordering my steps. I prayed that the Lord would have taken my flesh out of the way of the decision that was being made for my son's rehabilitation facility and allowed it to be the place and decision from the Lord. I had begun to feel that I was making things more difficult with my decisions. There were so many times that I had said that I would put the situation in the Lord's hand, but I found that I would take it upon myself to pick the situation up again. I realized that the walk that I was taking was a spiritual walk, and I wanted to give it back to the Lord.

Just when I turned it all over to the Lord, I received a phone call from the caseworker of the hospital to inform me that the rehabilitation center that had turned my son down earlier in the week had called her back to inform her that their staff had agreed to accept my son as a patient in their facility. As soon as I got off the phone with that caseworker, I felt so relieved. I felt such a peace of mind, my body felt so calmed down, and I began to thank God because I realized that was my confirmation from the Lord to confirm that Mount Vernon was the place for my son. As I sat there praying, the Lord spoke to me and said, "You were praying for the facility that was best for LaRicko, but at the same time, you wanted him to stay here in the city limits close to you for his rehabilitation." But the Lord reminded me that I was concerned about what was best for me because I wanted him near me, but LaRicko didn't need me; he needed the Lord, and the Lord directed us to that rehabilitation center that was four hours away, which was the best for my son. There's so many times in life we pray and ask God for certain blessings, and when he gives it to us, just because it did not come the way we wanted it or it didn't happen the way we expected it to happen, we miss our chances in life, or we take the long road when it was not necessary. God doesn't always show up how we want him to, but just know he knows what's best for us. Even if we don't realize that, our father (God) knows.

For I know the thoughts that I think toward you, saith the Lord, thoughts of peace, and not of evil, to give you an expected end. (Jeremiah 29:11)

I informed my brother, Horace, immediately that I was going to transfer LaRicko to Mount Vernon because I felt really good about the idea. I explained to Horace the issues that my son and I had encountered the past weeks at the hospital, which was allowing me to know that we weren't making the right decision to stay here in the city limits. And when I was done explaining the situation to my brother, he was okay with the idea, but at the same time, he wasn't comfortable with the thought that LaRicko was going to be so far away from us; neither was I. But my brother felt that if I was going to try the facility out, he was going to be supportive of my decision. My brother, Horace, was always on the phone checking on LaRicko and me all day long, so I knew that he would support on whatever decision that I made.

Chapter 6

My Faith under Pressure!

While I was at the hospital, the nurse came in and said to me that they were going to be moving my son to another room because they had a patient that was in worse condition than my son and the patient needed to be in the room right at the nurses' station. So I began to pack up LaRicko's personal things and started transferring them down the hall where he was being moved. I felt pretty good about that because we didn't have to be there much longer. As we settled into LaRicko's new room, I continued to have concerns about the bruises that were on his legs because the bruises didn't appear to be getting any better at that point.

It was the weekend again, and I was sitting there at the hospital with my son as I usually did, and a while later, his dad came up to the hospital to visit with LaRicko. Well, while his dad was there, LaRicko had begun to look as if he was trying to sit up again. So Chester stood on one side of LaRicko's bed and I stood on the other side, and we placed our hands slowly behind LaRicko's back, and I said to LaRicko, "We're going to sit you up on the count of three, and I counted, "One . . . two . . . three," and we began to sit LaRicko up. While he was in a sitting position, he said, "This feels so good!" His dad and I were so excited until our son began to get a bit aggravated, and his dad had begun to get so sad and wanted to leave the hospital. LaRicko's dad didn't realize that it was a blessing that all those things were beginning to happen, being that we had been told that our son was completely brain-dead. As that evening went on, I prayed with my son as well as talked to him until he calmed down. And after a while, LaRicko fell asleep. So I headed home for the evening and prepared for church the next day.

After I left church, I headed to the hospital to visit with my son, and after I was there talking to him, I began to comb LaRicko's hair and share with him about the church services. As I was standing there, my son asked me, "Mom, what's wrong with me?" I was so thankful to God. I began to tell LaRicko what happened to him. And shortly afterward, LaRicko's brother, Michael, called, and I told Michael that LaRicko had asked me what was wrong with him. Mike could hardly believe it. I asked LaRicko if he wanted to talk to Michael on the phone, and LaRicko said yes. So I put the phone to LaRicko's ear, and he and Michael began to talk. I was so happy because God had showed up and was showing out! That ended up being our miracle weekend.

That Monday passed, and I began counting down the days because we were going to be leaving the hospital on that Thursday headed for Mount Vernon.

The next day while I was at work, I received another phone call from the hospital informing that my son would be going into surgery to have a PIC line placed in the upper part of his arm, being that his IV tube continued to come out of his arm. And needless to say, I was very upset on one hand because I felt why wasn't I informed sooner that the surgery was going to be taking place so that I could have been at the hospital already? And I could not believe that the staff had allowed my son to have been poked in his arms so many times, and he had all kinds of bruises on his arm, and finally, prior to him being transferred to another facility, the staff decide to perform that procedure. So right away, I left my job and rushed to the hospital, getting there as they were placing LaRicko on the bed to take him to surgery. I leaned over and kissed LaRicko and said, "I love you," and I let him know that I was there and I would be waiting for him as soon as he got back from surgery.

As the staff began to roll LaRicko in his bed down the hall on the way to surgery, I stood in the doorway of his room and watched my son until he was out of my sight. Then I walked over to a chair that was sitting in LaRicko's hospital room and sat down and began to pray. I was thinking to myself that LaRicko's illness has truly been a rough walk for me. I prayed, "Lord, there had been a time that I wanted to give up, but, Lord, you showed me where I need to hold on a while longer." I continued to pray that I just trusted the Lord on the rest of that walk because I was just so numb with the whole situation right now. After I finished praying, I picked up the phone and called to talk to my parents regarding LaRicko being in surgery to have a PIC line placed in his arm, and my mother said that was a good thing because once that procedure was done, the nurses wouldn't have to continue to move the IV tubes in LaRicko's arms anymore. So that sounded great to me. I was just disappointed that the doctor didn't take advantage of the procedure sooner.

After sitting in LaRicko's room for almost an hour, I looked down the hall, and what did I see? The nurses bringing my son back to me. I was so happy that the surgery went well. My son was just lying there with his eyes open, staring straight ahead. He did not sleep through that whole procedure. But he appeared to be okay. Of course, I leaned over the bed rails and kissed LaRicko as I began to talk to him again about going to Mount Vernon so that we could start looking forward to him getting better. We were beginning to count down the days for us to head to Mount Vernon. The caseworker told me that we would be transferring my son to Mount Vernon on the eighteenth of September. Believe it or not, I couldn't wait to leave that hospital; the only thing was, I just didn't want LaRicko four hours away from me, but at least he would be away from that hospital. But from the looks of the whole situation, Mount Vernon appeared to be the best facility for LaRicko.

As I was sitting in LaRicko's room spending time with him as always, my phone rang, and it was a friend of mine who had been in our lives for a very long time. My friend BJ wanted to know how LaRicko was doing. And I had begun to share with him that I was going to be transferring my son to Mount Vernon, which was a rehabilitation center, and BJ was very happy to hear that. BJ asked me if there was anything that LaRicko needed to go to the new facility that could help to make his recovery a successful one. So I began to share with BJ all the things that were on the list of papers that the facility sent to me to inform me of all the things *that they wanted us to bring for LaRicko. After sharing that information with BJ, he suggested he would come by the hospital and pick me up so that we could go and shop for my son. So after I hung up the phone from speaking with BJ, I turned to LaRicko and informed him that BJ and I were going to go shopping for him and that I would back shortly. I kissed LaRicko, told him I loved him, and headed to the store with BJ. By the time I had walked down to the front door of the hospital, BJ drove up and picked me up, and we headed to the store. I could not believe all the things that BJ purchased for my son. BJ had purchased everything that LaRicko needed, from sweatpants, sweatshirts, T-shirts, socks; he even bought him some hair clippers to cut his hair and things to shave with. It was such a blessing how BJ just showed up and purchased everything my son needed and more. I just thanked God for BJ; he had truly been such a blessing in our life.*

When I returned to the hospital, I walked into my son's room, and his eyes were still open, so I began to take things out of the bags to show LaRicko all his new things that BJ had purchased for him that he would be taking to Mount Vernon. Shortly afterward, LaRicko's fiancée walked into the room, and I began to show her all the things that were purchased as well. She was excited about everything. My son's fiancée sat down and began to write LaRicko's name inside all his clothes and socks, which was something that I would have never thought about doing. LaRicko's fiancée said when LaRicko gets to Mount Vernon, the staff would be able to recognize his personal items because the items will have LaRicko's name written in them. I thanked God for my son's fiancée as well because she was such a positive young lady, and that was exactly what we needed in our lives especially with the condition that we were dealing with.

After sitting there with my son and his fiancée a little while longer, I decided to head home and began to pray for a much better day for my son to come tomorrow.

On my way home from the hospital, I stopped by the store to pick up some thank-you cards to address to all the staff at the hospital that had assisted us with my son. We had been at that hospital for so long that I felt that I knew all the staff personally. I felt that we had been at their facility for so long that expressing my appreciation through a card was the least that I could do. After leaving the store, I continued home where I would always take time out to spend time with the Lord in my place that I have always referred to as my comfort zone. Shortly after my praying, I began to address the thank-you cards for the staff at the hospital. As I sat down and began to go through my daily journal that I kept faithfully through my son's illness, I wrote down every name that was written in my journal because the names were of the people that assisted my son during our stay at the hospital. I made sure that I thanked every one of them personally with a card. When I was done with addressing the cards, I began to prepare myself for bed, counting down the days for the trip to Mount Vernon.

The next day when I got to the hospital, I couldn't wait to share with several of the nurses that my son talked over the weekend. That was really a joke to them because the doctor said that there was no way that LaRicko could possibly talk with the tracheotomy in his throat. I began to tell the staff what my son had said to me and his dad over the weekend, and the staff began to chuckle in disbelief. As the word traveled over the floor of the hospital that I was saying that my son talked, nurses and technicians as well as a couple of doctors came into LaRicko's room *and began to question me on what LaRicko had said. I began to tell them the different things LaRicko had said to me, and they stood around in LaRicko's room and began to stare at my son because they just knew I was making that up. So I began to talk to my son while the staff was standing there, and I asked him to say hello or something to them so that they would know that I didn't make that story up. Well, of course LaRicko wouldn't say anything, and the staff began to look at me as if I had lost my mind. After the staff had been standing around and chatting for a while, they decided to leave us alone. And they said to me, "We wish you luck and hope that your son would eventually get better." I thanked them for all that they'd done for us, and told them, "We'll be back to see you once LaRicko gets out of rehab." As the staff left LaRicko's room, I felt that I knew what they were thinking: what's wrong with me. And I thought to myself, Why didn't my son say something, so that the staff would have known that what I was saying was true? But LaRicko would not say a word. I began to pray that the Lord would please show those people in that hospital that he was in the miracle-working business. I continued to pray to the Lord with "I already know what you can do, and I know you are going to bring us out of the situation that we were in, but show the unbelievers at that hospital. I want the staff to see our miracle before we leave the hospital tomorrow."*

Then shall thy light break forth as the morning, and thine health shall spring forth speedily: and thy righteousness shall go before thee: the glory of the Lord shall be thy reward. (Isaiah 58:8)

On our last night at the hospital, one of the nurses who had been caring for LaRicko from the very beginning when LaRicko was moved down to the second floor of the hospital was his nurse for the evening.

So as I was sitting at my son's bedside, the nurse walked into LaRicko's room, and she said to me, "I heard that your son is talking." I said, "Yes, he is." As she began to take LaRicko's blood pressure, she started talking to him. She said, "LaRicko, I heard that you could talk, but I don't believe it because you haven't said a word to me all day." And LaRicko was just lying there, showing no reaction. Well, sitting on LaRicko's table, there was an oscillating fan in his room, which the nurses had placed there for my son because he was always perspiring. As the nurse was caring for him, she said, "LaRicko, I'm going to have to move your fan over a little bit, is that okay?" There was still no response from LaRicko. And then the nurse moved the cover from my son so that he'd continue to be cool during her procedure. After a while, the fan began to blow LaRicko's gown up, and she took his gown and pulled it down. As she turned around and began to do other things to him, she noticed that his gown had blown up again, so she asked him, "LaRicko, are you pulling your gown up, or is the fan blowing it up?" And LaRicko said, "It's the fan." The nurse said, "Oh my god! Did he just talk?" The nurse just about passed out. I was standing there with tears in my eyes because I prayed that the Lord showed up for me before we left the hospital the next day because the people just did not believe me. "Thank you, Jesus," I said. And needless to say, the nurse went out into the hallway and began to tell the staff, "He really did talk." And some of the staff was still saying that my son couldn't be talking with that tracheotomy in his throat. The staff said there was no way that LaRicko's vocal box could even operate with that tracheotomy in his throat, which is not even possible. I said, "With my God, all things are possible."

I can do all things through Christ which strengtheneth me. (Philippians 4:13)

Several people began to come back to LaRicko's room and just stared at him in disbelief, but I thanked God that he allowed at least one of the nurses at the hospital to hear LaRicko talk before we left that hospital. Praise the Lord.

Praise ye the Lord. O give thanks unto the Lord; for he is good: for his mercy endureth for ever. (Psalm 106:1)

On the fifty-fourth day in that hospital, the time had finally come for us to move to another level. While we were waiting for the ambulance drivers, the staff began to prepare my son for the long four-hour journey. As that was going on, I went up to the intensive care unit to thank everyone personally as well as hand each one of them a thank-you card for the service that they had given to me and my son. They all were so surprised and began to hug me and wished me and my son good luck. As I walked away from the unit, I walked to other areas of the hospital and handed out thank-you cards to the staff that had supported us also. Then I began to walk down to the floor where my son was being prepared for our departure and began to hand out thank-you cards to each one of the hospital staff on that floor as well. They all appeared to be so teary eyed as we were gathering our things together to head for the next facility.

The time had come when the doctor would come in to talk to me. As the doctor stood on one side of my son's bed and I stood on the other side, the doctor said to me, "This is my final say to you. Your son's diagnosis is he is completely brain-dead, and there will be absolutely no changes in his condition." The doctor included that maybe in two to three years from now, he may be able to get off the ventilator. There was no guarantee that this would happen, but he definitely would remain a vegetable for the rest of his life. So as I stood there, I said, "Okay, and I'd like to thank you for all you've done for him, and we will see you when we get back." And of course, I got the same look from the doctor as I got from everyone else. She's crazy! As I told them earlier, I am crazy enough to believe that the Lord is going to heal him because I know that with my God, all things are possible.

And Jesus looking upon them saith; With men it is impossible, but not with God: for with God all things are possible. (Mark 10:27)

Here we go. They had my son all prepared to go to Mount Vernon, and we were walking down the hallway—LaRicko's dad (Chester), my son's aunt Lela, my son's fiancée, and I. All the staff began to wave at us as we were leaving. I began to talk to my son as I was walking beside him while they were rolling him in the bed to the ambulance. At all times I'd let him know that I was there and assured him that I wasn't going to leave him.

After we got outside and they began to place LaRicko in the ambulance, I asked the ambulance driver if it was okay that I could ride in the ambulance with them. I was informed by the driver that only the medical team could ride with them in the ambulance. Of course, I didn't take no for an answer. I began to pray as they were positioning all the oxygen and other things that my son needed for the trip in the ambulance. I stood and watched as they were doing all the hookups and plug-ins to assure that LaRicko was okay, and I asked again, "Who can I talk to regarding riding with my son in the ambulance? I want him to hear my voice so that he'd know I'm here with him." The ambulance driver said to me, "its okay, you can ride in here with us." Once again, there's my God, showing up again!

Thou Lord, will bless the righteous; with favour wilt thou compass him as with a shield. (Psalm 5:12)

Being that I had gotten the approval to be able to ride in the ambulance from the driver, I walked to the front passenger side door and got in. I placed my purse on the floor, and I turned around to look behind me to see how close I was to my son. That was great because LaRicko could hear my voice so that I can assure him that I'm here with him. As we began to drive off, I was just praying in my spirit, "Lord, I trust you that we are headed to the right place for LaRicko." I knew that this was God because I didn't feel my strength anymore; I knew that God was carrying me. I began to remember the poem, "Footprints in the Sand." After a long rough road of one issue after another, it appeared that it was only one set of footprints. There's times when it seemed as if you were all alone, and we question, "Lord, where are you?" But the Lord is actually saying, "I'm here, I am carrying you." And that gave me comfort the more I thought about it in that way.

As we pulled away from the hospital parking lot, I began to look back at the hospital and felt a bit sentimental, but I knew it was time for us to go. I began to talk to the ambulance driver as we were leaving while looking back at my son lying there on the ambulance stretcher, and the paramedic was sitting on one side of him, holding this odd piece of medical tool, which, every few minutes, he had to use to literally pump oxygen into my son's tracheotomy. I could hardly believe my eyes. I hadn't thought about the fact that the ambulance did not have the same setup as the hospital. So I'm thinking to myself that the paramedic was going to have to pump oxygen in my son for over four hours. I was really putting that whole situation in God's hands. My baby was actually going to be more than three hundred miles away from me. I was just praying. That was **God's grace to a mother's prayer!**

As we traveled down the highway, I kept looking out of the rearview window as well as watching my son in the back, because in the car behind us was LaRicko's dad, his aunt Lela, and his fiancée, and I wanted to make sure that they were keeping up with the ambulance. After about a couple hundred miles down the road, I just happened to look over at the driver, noticing that there was an eighteen wheeler next to us, and as I continued to watch the eighteen wheeler, I noticed that it was getting closer and closer to the driver's side door of the ambulance, and I said to the ambulance driver, "Look, he is going to run us off the road." The ambulance driver was listening to his music and was not paying any attention to the truck at all. As soon as I said that, thank God the ambulance driver was able to pull quickly to the shoulder of the road, jerking the steering wheel really quick, and we swerved off the road. I turned to look back at my son and the paramedic with hopes that everything was going okay, and I saw where the paramedic seemed to have been a bit nervous, and I yelled back to my son, "Baby, everything is okay. Momma's here, don't worry." I always felt that as long as LaRicko could hear my voice that he'd relax better. My son's dad called me on my cell phone in a panic, wanting to know what was going on with the ambulance driver that he didn't notice what was going on sooner that he had to go off the road like that. So I informed him that the driver didn't notice the truck until I said something to him. The driver thanked me for getting his attention because he said he was just enjoying the music and concentrating on the road ahead of him, not *even noticing the eighteen wheeler truck beside him. So needless to say, he remained focused after that terrible scene. I was thankful that I was blessed to ride in the ambulance.*

As we continued down the road, I began to pray, and I couldn't help but think that the enemy was still trying to take my son from me. The enemy knew that we were headed for a better place for my son's recovery, and he was trying to destroy us before we got there. I thanked God that he allowed me to ride in the ambulance with them because it was obvious that the driver wouldn't have ever noticed until it was too late. Going up to Mount Vernon, we were in mountains and hills all the way, and if the truck had run over the ambulance, it would have easily ran off one of those deep hills down in a valley—need I say more? I began to say, "Thank you, Lord, for watching over us."

The Lord said, I will never leave you nor forsake thee. (Hebrews 13:5)

As I said, my faith was truly under pressure!

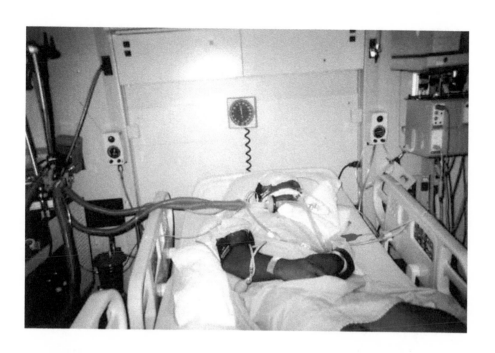

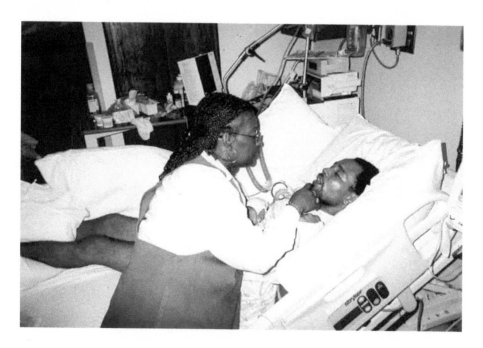

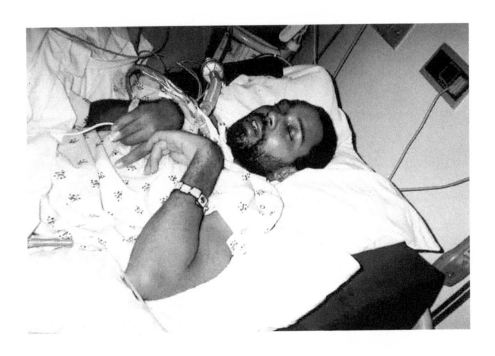

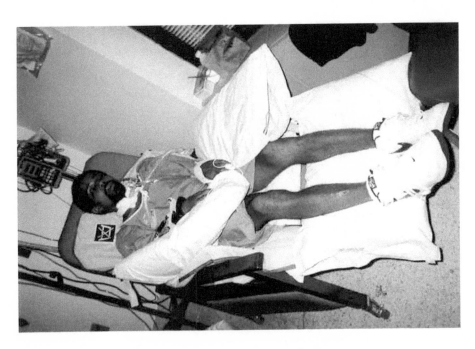

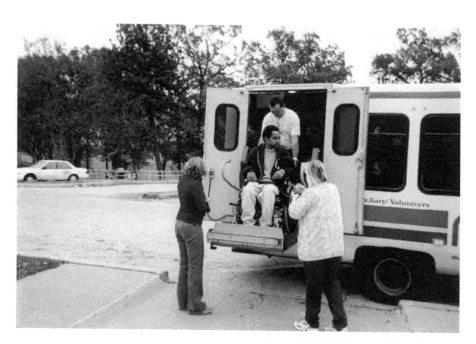

Chapter 7

Moving to another Level

*H*ere we were four hours later at
the rehabilitation center where my son was going to be for a while.
Lord knows I didn't know what to think about that whole thing; I was
just trusting God to be ordering my steps. As the paramedics began to
take LaRicko out of the ambulance, I stood there watching along with
LaRicko's dad, his aunt Lela, and LaRicko's fiancée, praying and asking
myself why were we in that situation. I just can't believe that my entire
life had changed in a matter of minutes. I have seen things that I'd never
thought I'd see in the pothole situation that I was in. It was as if I had
fallen into a deep hole and just couldn't find my way out, and all I had
to hold on to was my faith.

As the paramedics entered the elevator, we followed behind them, and I had on my brave face, not knowing what to expect next. The paramedic pressed the number to the floor where we needed to get off, and I could hardly wait to see what that area of the facility was going to look like. And when the elevator doors opened, we were all the way on the opposite end of the facility from where I'd already visited. But as we walked to the other side, it all became familiar. The head nurse came out and introduced herself to all of us as she signed the needed documents to transfer my son there. The nurse was very nice to us as she showed us to the area where the paramedics transferred LaRicko from the ambulance stretcher over to the new facility's bed.

As the time went on, the nurse introduced us to the staff, which was there at the time of LaRicko's arrival, and informed us that the nurse needed to ask me some further questions as she lead us back out to the lobby area. Shortly afterward, one of the nurses came out with several documents on a clipboard. She introduced herself and made us feel so comfortable about the whole thing. She began to ask several questions as well as informing us of all the convenient things that they had at the facility. The nurse also asked me if my son could talk, and I told her that he'd said a few words at the hospital, but he was still in a coma, and the doctor said that LaRicko would never be anything but a vegetable. And I continued to say to the nurse that I had still prayed that LaRicko would walk out of their facility. The nurse smiled as she agreed with me. I thought to myself that things were going to be better than I thought. So after the nurse finished with all her questions, she said to us that if we'd like to go out and get something to eat, we should feel free because it was going to take quite of bit of time to get all the medical equipment changed on my son. They had to change out the tube in LaRicko's throat, stomach, cathedra, and the IV tubes. They actually had to take off all the equipment that the hospital had attached to him and change it all to their facility's equipment. As they were doing all those things, the nurse also made me aware of a couple of bedsores that my son had on his backside, which had gone untreated at the hospital. I was so sad about that, but I thanked God that we made it there in time so that those sores can be treated before they'd gotten any worse. I wanted to stay in the area while the staff were changing all those things on LaRicko because that was a new area, and I wanted to make sure that LaRicko was okay, but everyone else was kind of hungry, and we were told that the facility had a cafeteria downstairs, so we all decided to take advantage of that.

While we were downstairs in the cafeteria, we also ran into several nice people, and now I'm feeling that this was the right place for my son. But I couldn't wait to get back upstairs where my son was to make sure things were going well. As I walked back into the area where my son was, I noticed the curtains had been drawn, so of course I couldn't see LaRicko, but the nurses were talking back and forth, and I actually heard my son say, "You are hurting me!" The nurse said to LaRicko, "Shut up," so I stood there for a few more minutes just to make sure that I was not misunderstanding what was really going on. And Chester and LaRicko's aunt Lela didn't want me to be upset when I asked what was going on, because that was where LaRicko was going to be for a while, and we really didn't want to cause any problems. That nurse obviously assumed we were going to be gone for a while, but little did she know I was anxious to get back to my son. Then I heard LaRicko say, "Stop hitting me!" **Wow!** *All of a sudden, that comfortable feeling that had built up in my spirit was suddenly taken away. I asked from the other side of the curtain, "Do you all want me to come and talk to him?" The nurses were quiet for a minute because they were stunned that we were back so soon, and slowly one of them answered me with* *a no. A few seconds later, I heard my son say again, "You are hurting me!" Of course, I rushed around the curtains to see what was going on, and I saw my son trying to swing his weak retarded-looking arms, which hadn't moved in fifty-four days. He was so upset. I tried to calm him down because I knew something was going wrong for him to react like that. And through all that, I noticed LaRicko was really beginning to talk more. I said to LaRicko, "Momma's here" because I knew my son still couldn't see me. And my son said to me, "Mom, she hit me," and I really was upset. Of course the nurse said that it wasn't true, but I knew my son would not lie about something such as that, so I immediately went to the nurses' station to get the head nurse of the facility. I was having second thoughts all the way to the office; did I just make a mistake by bringing my son here or what? But needless to say, I prayed and kept the faith. At that point, I was looking to the hills from whence comes my help, and I knew that all my help comes from the Lord.*

I will lift up mine eyes unto the hills, from whence cometh my help. My help cometh from the Lord, which made heaven and earth. (Psalm 121:1-2)

Because I knew how hard it was to get my son to that facility, I couldn't possibly just take him from there and have him transferred somewhere else too easily. So I was talking to myself, trying to remain calm. As the head nurse came out to check things out, she allowed me to stand right there with her while she began to ask questions. The head nurse wanted to assure me that those kinds of issues are zero tolerance at that rehabilitation center. She informed me that if that nurse did hit my son, it would be that nurse's last day employed by the facility. The head nurse made sure that she investigated the whole situation; she began to talk to each person regarding what happened in that room behind those pulled curtains. And needless to say, for the rest of our visit at the facility, we never saw that nurse again, and I didn't concern myself with where she was as long as she was not with my son. I just prayed that she'd find it in her heart to never hurt anyone else's loved one. People were in that facility for rehabilitation, not to be upset or tortured. And as I was approaching our first day there, I was still reminded of the hospital that we had just left; there were so many uncaring people, and I didn't need to feel that way at the new facility because we had a very long road to travel for LaRicko's recovery. So as that afternoon went on, there were other nurses, who were very nice and supportive, that were brought in and introduced to us.

As the evening went on, LaRicko's dad and his aunt Lela prepared them-selves for the four-hour drive back home. Before LaRicko's dad left, he walked over to LaRicko and began to talk to him. My son always had love for dogs, and he truly got that from his dad. Somehow, LaRicko and his dad began discussing dogs, and he asked his dad if he'd get him a dog when he got out of rehab, and his dad said yes. That appeared to cheer LaRicko up a little bit, and as his dad began to walk out of LaRicko's room, LaRicko asked, "Dad, are you going to get me a dog, for real?" And his dad turned back and said to him, "I promise you, I will get you a dog." My son had made a 360-degree turn in a matter of hours. That was awesome. LaRicko was talking through that tracheotomy, and the doctors and nurses back at the hospital said it could not be done.

Later on that evening, while his fiancée and I sat around in LaRicko's room, the head nurse for the facility came in and spoke to us and apologized to us again for what happened earlier, and of course, we accepted her apology; she asked us if we'd like to stay in the room with LaRicko all night. The nurse said that she wanted us to observe everything and everyone because she didn't want us to think that the behavior from the other nurse earlier was allowed there. Even though his fiancée and I had paid for our rooms across the way, we decided to sit and be assured that LaRicko was being taken of properly. So the staff brought in big comfortable recliners, one for me and one for his fiancée. I was a bit concerned for LaRicko's fiancée's comfort because she was pregnant with my first grandbaby, but one thing I can say about her was that she was truly a strong and positive young lady. And that was just what we needed.

It was so amazing as that day went on. My parents called to check on us, and my son talked to my mother on the phone. When he heard her voice, he said, "Hey, Grandma." He already knew who she was, and my brother, Horace (Baba), called as well, and my son said, "Hey, Uncle Baba." That was truly amazing because LaRicko was still in a coma and knew who everyone was. LaRicko could not see us, but he could hear everything and was able to talk. That was really an odd experience for me. **God is truly amazing!**

The evening was still a bit young, and LaRicko began to talk as if he was stranded on the side of the road. That was interesting because a few months prior to his illness, his fiancée's car did break down on the side of the road, and it was as if he was reliving that entire incident. His fiancée and I tried to let LaRicko know that he was not on the side of the road; he was in the hospital, and when we told him that, he tried his best to get out of bed. He was so upset by that. He kept saying, "I don't like hospitals, get me out of here!" After a while, a male nurse came into the room, and my son said to the nurse, "Can you help me?" and the nurse said, "Sure, Ricko, what do you need?" And LaRicko said to him, "We're stranded on the side of the road, can you call a tow truck?"

It was beginning to become a bit comical because the nurse began to joke back and forth with LaRicko. The nurse told my son that he'd go get his pickup truck and come back and pull their car home for him, and LaRicko thanked him several times for offering to do that for us. That whole day had just been an interesting experience for us. We had seen such an awesome change in my son in one day. **God is showing up and showing out!** *So the rest of the night, we sat in LaRicko's room watching the nurses come in and out, caring for him. After a very upsetting afternoon, the rest of the day turned out to be such a blessed one. After several hours of sitting, his fiancée and I fell asleep. And each time someone came into the room, I'd wake up to see what was going on. That went on all night long, so needless to say, I was very tired the next day.*

The next day was LaRicko's fiancée's birthday, and she was right there by his side. That day started out being very good because the doctor that was going to be caring for my son during his stay came into LaRicko's room at approximately 9:21 a.m. He introduced himself to us, and he had several other assistants with him to help with all the things he was getting ready to do for my son. The doctor walked over and looked at LaRicko and looked at the tracheotomy in his neck, and he ordered one of his assistants to place a voice box piece to my son's tracheotomy so the doctor could hear LaRicko's voice better. After putting the piece in place, the doctor began to ask LaRicko questions. The first one he asked LaRicko was his name, and my son told him; and then he asked my son, "LaRicko, how do you feel?" My son said, "My heart is hurting" as LaRicko began to cry, and the doctor asked him to show him where his heart was hurting, and my son said to him, "My heart is hurting emotionally." I was so surprised at that answer. As the doctor continued to ask LaRicko questions, he looked at me and said, "He's going to be fine." The doctor included that LaRicko would recovery at least 85 percent. All of the staff was standing around LaRicko's bed, waiting to follow the doctor's orders, as he continued to ask LaRicko more questions. After evaluating my son a bit further, the doctor said to me, "He should be okay in a couple of weeks or so." My heart rejoiced! "Thank you, Lord," I said. So that was the best place for my son. My prayers had been answered. My son had been on the ventilator for a couple months, and the doctor told his assistants to turn off the oxygen, and that's what they did. I stood there praying and looking, as if to say, I hope that doctor knows what he is doing. As the staff was turning all those equipments off, it got so quiet in the room, and I'm looking at my son to notice his reaction, and my son was okay for a little while. I was surprised because again, I was told at the hospital that we left from yesterday that LaRicko would never survive without the ventilator, and here the doctor was taking my son off for minutes at a time. As the morning went on, things began to get even better because my son had been lying on his back for the past fifty-four days, and now, fifty-five days later, the doctor ordered for the nurses to sit LaRicko up in a chair. It was so amazing to see how they lifted him up out of the bed with a crane and placed him down in a chair. After LaRicko was sitting up for a little while, I wanted to take a picture of him sitting there because I was excited to see him looking alive again, so I asked him if I could take a picture of him and his fiancée, and he began to cry because he did not want me to take a picture of him. I assured him that I wouldn't take a picture if he didn't want me to. And I sat down and began to talk to him to see why he was so sad so that I could share with him how blessed he really was. At that point, I explained to my son that he didn't have any reason to be sad. His fiancée and I began to share with LaRicko what had been going on with him for the past fifty-four days. LaRicko actually thought he had been in a car accident, but we shared with him what the doctors said had happened to him. I didn't know if he really understood what we were saying, but it appeared that he did. LaRicko just didn't know I was so happy with everything that I was seeing at the time because less than twenty-four hours ago, I was told by the doctor at the hospital that he would never be anything but a vegetable and to expect absolutely no changes in his condition. And hours later after we left the hospital, there was such a positive change in my son's condition. So with seeing all that, I was very excited!

The doctor that was caring for my son came in on Saturday morning to see him; to my amazement, the nurses informed me that the staff could not believe that the doctor would come in on a weekend. He had never come in on a weekend nor had he been on call for a weekend as long as he's been at that facility. And he had been on staff at the facility for over twenty years. The nurses included that the doctor was so impressed with LaRicko's conversation that he wanted to get started on his procedures as soon as possible. I smiled and thanked God for that confirmation to continue to hold on a while longer. Praise the Lord for favor.

Once the doctor came to LaRicko's room, he began to check LaRicko's vital signs, and he decided to take him off the ventilator again. I noticed that the doctor began to have the staff come in and begin to measure LaRicko's arms, because they were contracted in a locked position toward my son's chest, and then they measured LaRicko's hands, because they were contracted at the wrist, completely turned under, so that they can size him up for braces that would help straighten those areas out. And then they began to measure LaRicko's legs so that the staff could order him a wheelchair. Things were getting to be really exciting because I felt such a positive vibe from the doctor. And it was even better because the staff allowed my son's fiancée and me to stay in the room the entire time with LaRicko during that process to assure us that the doctors and nurses there were not inconsiderate people and that they were concerned about us being comfortable with them. Less than a week later—five days later, to be exact—after we had left the hospital, the doctor ordered the nurses to turn the ventilator off LaRicko at 8:25 a.m. and did not order them to turn it back on until 8:25 a.m. the next morning. The doctor was so pleased with how well LaRicko had done with it off, but he did not want to push things too fast by keeping him off for more than one day at a time. The doctor was trying to build my son's lungs back up to handle breathing on his own. LaRicko appeared to be doing very well. He was having a little rough time breathing here and there throughout the day, but overall, I was still happy because LaRicko was making such great progress.

Later that afternoon, the nurses came in and sat LaRicko on the edge of the bed, where they decided to stand him up for about three minutes. It looked so good to see my son standing up again. The nurses stood on each side of my son, holding him up. That facility did not waste any time getting LaRicko back on his feet. But later on that night, my son was beginning to have such a rough time. He complained about a sore throat and wanted to get out of there and go home; he just didn't realize how serious his condition was being that he was in a coma. When one of the nurses came in and talked to LaRicko, and he began to talk back to her, the nurse thought he was so cute, so she began to sing to him to try and make him feel better in spirit. It was really cute because the nurse's singing really calmed LaRicko down, and she stood there and sang until he actually went to sleep.

On the next day while we were there, everything was pretty much a repeated day, except the nurse came in and got LaRicko up out of the *bed not only one time to stand up for three minutes, but they actually got him up three times and allowed him to stand for three minutes each time. All these things had taken place in approximately a week from the time he'd left the hospital. And as time went on, we saw the staff's support more and more each day. So we became so comfortable with the nurses and doctors there that I made plans to go back home on the weekend (Sunday), and my son's fiancée decided to stay the entire following week, but she went to her room that was right across the grounds from the facility and relaxed each day. Because during the week at the facility, visitors were not allowed to visit during the day because it was the time that the patients were focusing on rehabilitation, and they didn't want any distractions from any outsiders. So LaRicko's fiancée stayed for a week in Mount Vernon after I left, and she would go and visit with LaRicko in the evenings. Everyone there was so nice to her. I thanked God for LaRicko's fiancée every day because she stuck by him.*

LaRicko was yet in their intensive care area of the facility, but as that week went on, the doctor had him moved from the intensive care area to another floor, which meant LaRicko, was making some improvements. So when I came back up to visit LaRicko on the next weekend, I was so happy to see that he was on another floor, which meant he was progressing. But I was very concerned about the fact that the staff had LaRicko lying on such a high bed with a special type of mattress under him. I was told being that my son had bedsores on him, that type of mattress he was lying on was the best for him during the healing process. But LaRicko had been on a type of medication back at the hospital, which caused him to move around and kick uncontrollably constantly. He could not control his body, so I feared that he would fall out of bed if no one was watching him. The facility couldn't believe that my son was given that type of medication for so long back at the hospital,

*and not only that, it was given to LaRicko several times a day. So it was
a rough period for LaRicko, as well as my-self, watching his body go
through those strange movements from medication he should have not
been taking. And I was so fearful that my son was going to eventually
fall from the bed if no one was watching him. And the staff assured me
that LaRicko was being watched from a camera at their front desk. So
while I was there for the weekend, of course I stayed in the room with my
son the whole time. I sat in a chair beside his bed. On that night while
I was sitting there, LaRicko began to talk to me about several things
that took place in his life back when he was a little boy. It was very
interesting because he reminded me how I would not allow him to go out
and play in the streets as the other little boys in the neighborhood were
allowed to do. Being that was obviously something that had remained
on his mind, I explained to LaRicko that I didn't want him to play in
the streets with the other kids because I didn't want to take a chance of
him getting hit by a car. Then LaRicko said, "But the other kids made
fun of me, and they called me a punk." And I was wondering to myself
where all of those kinds of thoughts coming from? By that time, one of
the nurses walked into LaRicko's room, and I began to share with the
nurse what the conversation that LaRicko was having with me, and the
nurse explained to me that taking place with LaRicko was a good thing
because LaRicko was trying to come out of the comatose state that he
was in. The nurse continued, "Most of the time when a person comes out
of a coma, the mind goes all the way back to the past, and then it catches
up with the present." While the nurse was there, my son began to take
one of his hands up to his mouth, back and forth. Out of concern, I asked
the nurse again, "What is he doing now?" The nurse explained to me
that LaRicko thinks he's drinking something. The nurse went further to
say, "Don't worry because what is going on is great, because LaRicko's
brain is working hard on coming out of that coma." Praise the Lord!*

I will praise thee, O Lord with my whole heart; I will shew forth all thy marvelous works. (Psalm 9:1)

I saw that we were continuing to move to another level. So after the nurse left the room, LaRicko began to cry, and I asked him what was wrong, and he began to share with me that he didn't understand why he was going through those things. And I kept trying to convince him that he was doing great at that point. But of course, LaRicko could not understand that because he didn't realize at that point how bad his condition really had been. I thought it was very interesting that even though LaRicko was in a coma, he remembered our pastor by name. LaRicko said, "Mom, please call and ask Pastor to come and pray for me," and I promised him that I would that. After I assured him that I would, he stopped crying. And as LaRicko and I continued to talk, he asked me to pray with him right now, and that's when I sat by my son's bedside and began to pray with him. I was so happy that I could pray for my son and he could respond to me because before, I would pray, and LaRicko would just be lying there. Lord, I thank you so much.

Whatever you ask for in Prayer with faith you will receive. (Matthew 21:22)

So when the next day came for us to head back to St. Louis, I was still a bit uncomfortable about my son lying on such very high mattress, but I was assured by the staff that LaRicko would be okay. After a while, the nurses came in and sat LaRicko up in a chair for a few hours, and while he was sitting up, I told LaRicko that I was going to be leaving shortly going back home so that I could prepare for work the next day. And LaRicko began to show his sad face as he began to tear up, and I told him that we would be back to visit with him on the weekend. I wanted LaRicko to understand that I couldn't visit with him during the week because no outsiders were allowed to visit the patients during the day because of the rehabilitation sessions. But I shared with LaRicko that I would be back on Friday and that I would visit with him the entire time until that Sunday evening. Being that it made LaRicko very sad to know that I was going to be leaving, I told the nurse that I was going to leave while my son was asleep and not let my son know that I had left. The nurse informed me that was never a good idea because I should always tell LaRicko the truth even if it made him sad because it makes it harder on the patient's recovery when you try and keep things from them, especially if the patient was in a comatose state. "Don't try and confuse them," the nurse said. "Be honest with him and let him know that you will call him during the week and let him hear your voice." Because if LaRicko had woken up and I wasn't there, that would not have been fair to LaRicko, and we wouldn't know what type of effect it may have caused my son. So with that in mind, I talked to LaRicko to let him know that I was going to be leaving shortly, and when he looked as if he wanted to cry, I explained to him that there was a phone right next to his bed and that I would be calling him and talking to him all the time. I also included that the nurse would be holding the phone up to his ear so that he could talk to me. I asked the nurse to assure me that the staff would do that for LaRicko and I, being that LaRicko was still in a coma. Of course, he couldn't see anything, and LaRicko's hands weren't in any condition to hold anything. My son could not hold a piece of paper even if you placed it in his hands; he was so weak and crippled. So after talking to LaRicko about those things, he appeared to be better about me leaving. So as we prepared to leave, I kissed my son and told him how much I loved him and could hardly wait to get back to see him. He kind of smiled and kissed me back and told me he loved me back. That was such joyous moments for me to hear LaRicko finally say those words back to me again. So as I walked out of LaRicko's room, he appeared to be okay.

Needless to say, as we traveled down the highway headed back home, I was just a few miles down the road when I decided to test the nurses to see if they would really hold the phone for LaRicko so that he could talk to me, and as sure as I called, the nurse did hold the phone to LaRicko's ear so that he could talk to me. At that point, my son was still talking through the tracheotomy in his throat, which I was told repeatedly that it wasn't possible. That's why I knew that God was working another miracle. I didn't keep LaRicko on long on the phone; I just wanted to assure him that I was going to call him on the phone so that he could talk to me.

In the wee hours of the morning, while I was lying in my bed praying and thanking God for showing up and showing out, something came to my mind to pick up the phone and check on my son at around 3:00 a.m. So I picked up the phone and called the nurses' station to check and see how my son was doing to make sure he was resting okay, and to my surprise, the nurse that answered the phone informed me that my son had fallen out of the bed and that the staff wasn't aware of that until they looked at the camera at the front desk of the nurses' station and noticed LaRicko was on the floor. At that point, I wanted to explode! I had expressed my concerns regarding that happening, and I was assured by the staff that they would watch LaRicko closely, being that his mattress and bed was so high off the floor and he was having the uncontrollable movements. I did not feel comfortable about my son laying that high off the floor at all from the very beginning when I walked into his room. And what was amazing to me was that the nurse said it so calmly as if he couldn't have hurt himself, and I knew that those floors were concrete, that's why I was so concerned about him being up so high. But as we continued to talk, the nurse said, "He doesn't appear to be hurt, and tomorrow, we are going to put him on another floor so he can have a nurse that would sit beside LaRicko at all times and make sure that he won't fall again." Of course, that was a rough time for me because I wanted to know if LaRicko was not in some kind of pain from the fall. And with the tracheotomy in his throat, tubes in his stomach, and IV tubes in his arm, I was wondering if any of those things were detached from him during that fall or what.

So the next morning when I called to check on LaRicko, I was informed that he was complaining about back pain. Go figure! The nurse said that LaRicko was given some pain medicine for that. But overall, the nurse said my son was doing well. I'll never forget when a friend of mine named John called to ask me how was LaRicko doing, I began to vent to John regarding how the staff allowed my son to fall out of the bed, and John burst out into a laugh. I'm holding the phone as if saying, "How dare you laugh at my son falling out of the bed!" After John's laugh, he said, "That's great! That's probably the fall that will push him to get better even faster." I said, "You know what, you're right." I began to think, All things work together for the good.

And we know that all things work together for good to them that love God, to them who are the called according to his purpose. (Romans 8:28)

Things are not always as bad as they appear!

Well, the next couple of days, LaRicko's condition continued to get better and better regarding his breathing, being that he had been taken off the ventilator; at that point, the doctor felt that he was ready to be taken off the ventilator completely, so the staff took LaRicko off the ventilator and allowed him to stay off it. And while LaRicko was being monitored to see how well he was going to do, being that he had been off the ventilator for a couple days at a time, on October 1, the doctor removed the tracheotomy out of my son's throat completely. At that point, I was rejoicing because where the doctors had said that LaRicko would never be taken off the ventilator, which my son will never be able to breathe on his own; my God said something different. Praise the Lord once again.

I will bless the Lord at all times: his praise shall continually be in my mouth. (Psalm 34:1)

Well, when Friday finally came around again, I couldn't wait to get back to Mount Vernon to see my son without the tracheotomy in his throat. That was such a blessing for us. When I walked into my son's room, he was lying there on the bed while the nurse finished bathing him and putting his clothes on for the day. I spoke to LaRicko while his head was turned in the opposite direction looking toward the wall; he didn't turn around to look at me, but he said, "Hey, Mom." I knew he was doing great. He was still in a comatose state and never looked around at that point, but he recognized my voice. As the nurse began to sit LaRicko up, the nurse pointed out to me my son's wheelchair; I was so happy to see that. Who would have ever thought I would be happy that my son was in a wheelchair? When I first came to the facility, I saw so many patients rolling themselves down the hall in their wheelchairs, and I remembered praying to the Lord to someday see my son in that position. To me, that was a great big step to see. So when I saw LaRicko's wheelchair in his room, I watched the nurse place LaRicko in it, but being that LaRicko was still in a comatose state, the nurse had to strap him down in his chair because my son could not hold himself up because he did not have the strength to do so. And LaRicko could not roll the wheelchair himself, so one of us had to push him around. But of course, I was happy to see him sitting there in the wheelchair. I told my son that he looked really great without the tube in his throat, and he said, "Thanks, Mom," and the nurse chuckled and said, "But LaRicko need to get some meat on those little bones." I will never forget how LaRicko appeared to be focusing on the nurse while he was feeding him; the nurse had to take the tube that was still attached to LaRicko's stomach and pour his liquid food through the tube. As LaRicko was sitting there, he said, "I would have never thought I'd see someone feeding me through my stomach." I told my son that at the point that he was in, he was so blessed. As the day went on, LaRicko wanted to just sit in his room and listen to his CD player. I remember my son sitting there with the earphones on his ears, and he was crying and singing the Curtis Mayfield song "Back to Living Again." My brother, Horace (Baba), had given LaRicko that CD after he had moved to Memphis earlier in the year, and my son would listen to it all the time. My brother was determined for me to get a CD player and put that CD of Curtis Mayfield in it and place the earphones on my son's ears while he was back at the hospital. And sure enough, when I had done that, LaRicko appeared to be more relaxed as long as it was on his ears; and when I'd take them off his ears, LaRicko began to get a bit fretful. And now my son was listening to the CD as he was singing and crying. But all those reactions were positive to me, so I was okay with it. LaRicko was getting better by the day. At that point of my son's stay, there was a very sweet lady that would watch over him also, and LaRicko called her Granny. And Granny made sure that he was comfortable at all times. When LaRicko would complain about being cold, Granny actually micro waved his clothes or his blanket before putting them on him. Granny just loved LaRicko as if he was actually her grandson. And then LaRicko also had another sweet person that he referred to as his aunt, and she was exactly the same as Granny was with him. I thought that it was such a great blessing to be allowed to see even more that you didn't have to be the same race to be shown lots of love by another.

As the afternoon approached, the nurse came to us and asked if we wanted to take LaRicko outside, and I was excited. I said of course; being that he hasn't been outside in over two months, which would be great for him. And shortly after we went outside, my mother and brother, Horace, called and said that they were right around the corner from the facility. I was really happy because, to their surprise, we had LaRicko outside, pushing him around in a wheelchair. As soon as LaRicko heard my mom and my brother's voice, he knew exactly who they were. My family was really pleased with the facility and the condition that LaRicko was in. As we began to walk all around the area, my Mother and Horace could not believe all the recreational opportunities that were there.

My brother began to push LaRicko around in his wheelchair, and we all went to the little park area of the facility and sat down and began to enjoy the day laughing and talking. Most of all we were thanking God for showing up and showing out in our lives for my son. As time went on while we were still sitting outside, LaRicko said to the family, "I want to thank you all for being there for me, and thank you, Mom, for holding on." He began to cry in the midst of saying those things, and I asked him, "Why are you crying?" He said, "Mom, with what I've been through and to see the family was there with me such as now, these are tears of joy." And I thought to myself, Wow! God, you are so awesome!

As the evening went on, we had to take LaRicko back into the facility so that he could take his medication, and that was when I introduced my family to the inside of the facility. The staff was so nice and friendly to my mother and brother that it made them feel right at home. After LaRicko's medication, the nurse felt it was time for him to lie down after being outside for the first time for quite a few hours, so while LaRicko was lying down, Horace decided to sit in LaRicko's room and talk with him while the rest of the family went into the lobby and sat around and talked about how excited we were with LaRicko's progress. It ended up being such a wonderful and blessed day!

When it was time for my son to go to bed for the evening, Horace finally came out, and we all went over to our rooms and relaxed for the evening. I was so blessed to have my family with me and to watch God work a miracle on my son.

First thing the next morning, I got up and went to take my shower so that I could go over and spend time with my son early and allow the rest of the family to relax for a while longer, but my mother heard me moving around, and she got up as well. After that, we all began to get dressed so that we could see how well LaRicko was doing.

When we all got over to see LaRicko, the nurse had already gotten him up, bathed him, and he was sitting in his wheelchair, waiting for us to come over to see him. Of course, as soon as we could, we took him back outside. LaRicko really enjoyed the whole time spending it with his grandmother and uncle from out of town. LaRicko also appeared to be a little more alert than he was the day before. I would always watch his reactions and listen to his conversation closely. I also noticed that the uncontrollable body movement was still there, but it was not as bad as it was in the beginning. But we always made sure that LaRicko was completely strapped to his wheelchair. All that was okay because we were on our way through the valley, and God was with us through it all.

Yea, though I walk through the valley of the shadow of death, I will fear no evil: for thou art with me; thy rod and thy staff they comfort me. (Psalm 23:4)

I was so excited even more.

As that afternoon went on, my mother and brother had to get back on the road and head home before it got too late in the evening, and I felt that both of them were very surprised and happy with the condition that they found LaRicko in. So as we said our good-byes to my mother and brother, we began to spend a little more time with LaRicko until it was time for him to get his last feeding of the evening through his feeding tube. Afterward, we began to prepare to head home as well. So I hugged and kissed LaRicko and shared with him how much I loved him and informed him that I will see him on the upcoming weekend and I couldn't wait to see how well he would be doing at that time. Of course, it was never a happy time for him when we prepared to leave, but I'd always remind him that I will call constantly to check on him; and if he needed to talk to me, the facility would call me for him.

On October 6, it got a bit more exciting for me because a nurse called me from the facility about midmorning, and she informed me that she would be taking LaRicko to the doctor that day so that he could take a swallowing evaluation to make sure that it would be okay for him to start eating through his mouth. The test would also show how much he has come out of the coma. So I wanted to jump up and down with *that news because that meant that the doctor would be removing the tube out of his stomach soon, and LaRicko would be eating solid foods because he needed that really soon, being that he was so skinny that all his clothes were falling off him. I could hardly wait until the nurse called me back later in the day with the news of whether LaRicko had passed the test or not. A few hours passed, and I received a call from the nurse again, and she shared with me that LaRicko had done really well on the test, and they would have to make another visit to make sure that he was okay to assure that he would not choke if he ate solid foods, being that the muscles in his throat had been so relaxed for so long. I was happy to hear that LaRicko had done well on his first visit regarding the swallowing test.*

I'll never forget the Wednesday that I was getting ready to go to Bible class when my home phone rang, and it was LaRicko on the other end. I was ecstatic! The nurse dialed the phone for him to call me. LaRicko asked me what was I doing and I told him that I was getting ready to go to Bible class. He then asked me if I'd thank everyone in the church for praying for him. I was amazed at that! I told my son, "Of course, I'd be more than happy to share that." So after our conversation on the phone, you know I just thanked God for my steps to the right thing to have done and the right place to have taken my son, which was best for him.

I waited patiently for the Lord; and he inclined unto me, and heard my cry. He brought me up also out of a horrible pit, out of the miry clay, and set my feet upon a rock, and established my goings. (Psalm 40:1-2)

When I got to Bible class, my pastor allowed me the opportunity to share my story with the church. I shared with the congregation what the doctor's diagnosis was regarding LaRicko less than a month ago, which was that my son would remain a vegetable because he was completely brain-dead. I continued, "Right before I left to come to church for Bible class, my son called me and asked me to thank the congregation for praying for him." The congregation just began to applaud and praise God for the miracle that he had performed. I know when praises go up, blessings come down!

The next day came, and while getting ready for work, I stopped and made a phone call to check on my son, and the nurse answered and told me that LaRicko had a good night's rest. The nurse shared with me how everyone had been bragging on how well LaRicko was doing. The nurse said that LaRicko had been working so hard on his recovery. I was so proud to hear that kind of report and asked the nurse to let LaRicko know that I had called to check on him, that I loved him, and that I would call him later. She assured me that she would. So I began to pray and say to the Lord, "Whatever your will was for the day, just let it be done. I'm so thankful to you, Lord, for showing up in our lives, to be a blessing to others. I realize that my walk in life could be the only Bible that some people may read."

The nurses would always call and inform me of what LaRicko's day was going to consist of. The doctor had removed LaRicko's catheter tube from him, which would have allowed LaRicko to urinate on his own, but unfortunately, my son was not able to urinate, so the nurse had to take LaRicko to the urologist that day to be assured that the issue was going to correct itself in time. So at that point, LaRicko was dealing with another painful issue, but I knew that God was going to show up once again for us. I was praying that it didn't take too long before LaRicko could urinate because I knew that was going to be painful for him. And as the day went on, I checked back later with the nurse to find out how LaRicko's results came out. And I was told by the nurse that the doctor said LaRicko was fine, it was just going to take a little time, being that he had been relying on the catheter for such a long time. When I talked to LaRicko over the phone, he kept saying to me, "It hurts, Mom, when the nurse has to take my urine." And I was sad about that; all I could say to him was, "It's going to be okay, it will pass really soon," praying that the Lord would hurry and bless my son on that situation because I could see that my son had truly been a fighter, and I knew that the Lord was working it out for him.

The weekend came up again, and I was looking forward to see my son because each weekend that we visited LaRicko, I could see improvement more and more, which was always exciting. Prior to me getting to Mount Vernon to visit LaRicko, I had spoken to one of the nurses who informed me that LaRicko's feeding tube had been removed from his stomach, which meant my son was ready to start eating. Wow! It was really exciting to see LaRicko without tubes in my baby's stomach when I got there! All of that was in our past; thank you, Lord. Even though the tube had been taken out of LaRicko's stomach, he was still a bit down in the dumps because he could not urinate, and the nurse had to force urine from him, which was very painful. The nurse, who had to perform the task that day, was very sad as well because she didn't want to hurt him any further. So the nurse would wait as long as she could before she would perform the painful task on LaRicko. The nurse would measure LaRicko's stomach to check the centimeters to see if the task needed to be performed, and she would look as if she wanted to cry. And as we all sat around and talked in the sitting area, we were praying as well that LaRicko could urinate. That issue may not have appeared to be something serious, but it was very serious.

As the nurse began to push LaRicko's wheelchair toward the bathroom, his fiancée went along with him, and they had a bright idea to turn on the water in the bathroom and allow it to run continually to see if that could help LaRicko urinate prior to the nurse performing the painful task.

After LaRicko's fiancée, the nurse, and my son was in the bathroom for about ten minutes, the nurse came out with tears in her eyes and her hands were over her mouth. I looked up at her, and I thought something terrible had happened, but she said, "He did it." I asked, "Without any help from you?" She said yes with excitement in her voice, and we all jumped up and thanked God and applauded as if we had won the lottery or something. And actually, I felt as if I had won the best prize ever, being that the Lord blessed us to have my son around a while longer. That was the greatest feeling ever. Things were coming around for us—at God's timing, not our timing—and I thanked God for that so many times. And I remember, minutes later as LaRicko rolled out of the bathroom in his wheelchair, how he appeared to be looking at us crowded around in the sitting area, waiting on him to come out so that we could applaud for him. He said, "**God has shown up, and showing out on me!**" With tears in our eyes, we all were so excited and began applauding for him. That really was an enjoyable moment.

So as the weekend went on, we just enjoyed every minute with LaRicko, just sitting around and talking, noticing him and how much he's coming around out of the coma. I watched LaRicko as he tried to eat for the first time, and because of his hands being contracted completely under, every time he'd try to take food up to his mouth, his food would just drop from his spoon. His fiancée and one of the other house nurses would try and assist him just a bit because their goal was for the patients

to help themselves. That was a very good thing. After a few minutes of
LaRicko trying to eat with a regular spoon, the nurse remembered that
a special spoon was made for LaRicko, and she went to his room and
got the spoon, which was a complete surprise to me that they had made
a special spoon for my son. Even with the special-made spoon, it was a
bit difficult for LaRicko to handle it, but I was so excited just to see my
son trying to put food in his mouth after months of seeing all equipment
attached to him. That was actually a wonderful and blessed sight to see.
His granny (the nurse) and aunt (the nurse) made sure that LaRicko
got the opportunity to eat all the food he wanted because he was so
skinny; they wanted to get meat on LaRicko's bones, as they would say.
Of course, they started LaRicko on softer foods first, being that he'd
just gotten the tube removed from his stomach, and the doctor warned
to make sure that his throat was okay for the swallowing. And LaRicko
appeared to be doing very well with eating. Thank God!

Well, the time had come for us to head back to St. Louis once again,
and as we began to say our good-byes to LaRicko and the fun-filled
staff, LaRicko seemed to have been okay at that point, being that we
were going to be leaving. His granny (the nurse) said she was going
to be preparing a milk shake for LaRicko before he went to bed, and
my son was excited about that plan. What made things so much better
was that everyone was so nice to LaRicko, and I could see that he felt
comfortable enough with the nurses that it didn't bother him as much as
it had in the past that we had to leave him and head back home. And with
me knowing that, it made me feel a lot better about leaving my son as
well. And before we left, LaRicko had a request for his dad, which was
to make LaRicko some chili as he used to make for him back when he
was a little boy. LaRicko included that he wanted some corn bread with
the chili as well. I was a bit surprised about the request because I never

remembered chili with corn bread, but LaRicko said that his dad used to make it all the time for him. So LaRicko's dad promised to make chili the following weekend and bring it back to LaRicko. Afterward, LaRicko and the staff were excited about that thought because they all were looking forward to chili and corn bread on the upcoming weekend.

Here comes another week of looking forward to God showing up and showing out in our lives with LaRicko. I called the facility, as I always have done, to check on my son, and I spoke with one of his nurses. She shared with me that he had been having diarrhea. We weren't too surprised at that because the nurse seemed to think that LaRicko's system was experiencing that type of reaction because he hadn't had any solid foods for a while, and his system would have to adjust to solid foods. When I spoke with my son, he was also complaining about his stomach hurting. Of course I prayed for him, and I felt that the issue was coming from his system needing to adjust to the solid foods also. As that week went on, LaRicko kept experiencing the same issue. It had begun to bother him so much that he was beginning to say to me that he did not feel good. But I kept saying to my son that God did not bring us that far to leave us now. I kept encouraging my son to look on the upside of things. Sometimes it was hard for me to keep LaRicko focused because he was still a bit in a comatose state condition. But the people at the facility were such a great support group for LaRicko as well that I didn't worry much about the issue because I knew that the staff would take care of him.

When we got back to see LaRicko on the weekend, needless to say, everyone was looking forward to LaRicko's dad's famous chili and corn bread. Chester brought in the chili, and the staff placed it in the refrigerator until lunchtime, and needless to say, it was the talk of the *facility that weekend. How funny! That was so inspiring to LaRicko because he got first-class service as they prepared a room for my son to set up and serve his chili to everyone. That was fun for all of us!*

For the past couple of weeks or so, LaRicko had been in an area where he had to be watched at all times by a nurse. The nurse would sit in LaRicko's room throughout the night to assure that he was doing okay and to make sure he wouldn't fall out of the bed again. So I really was happy about that, but by the end of the week, I was informed that LaRicko was being moved to another area of the facility, which was advancement for him. And needless to say, I was concerned that LaRicko may not have been ready for such advancement so soon. But I had to once again let go of that thought and let God. It was around one month from the date that LaRicko had left the hospital when he was up in a wheelchair, and without any tubes attached to him as well as breathing on his own, that was truly a blessing. I received another call from the nurse to share with me that one of the staff members was going to be taking LaRicko to the optician because they felt that LaRicko's vision had gotten bad. The nurse felt that LaRicko needed to be tested for eyeglasses. I was okay with that because I thanked God that LaRicko was still alive. But later on that day after the visit with the optician, I was pleased to find that the doctor said that LaRicko just needed a little more time to overcome his illness because he was still slightly in a coma, and as he comes out of the coma, his sight should be okay.

A few days later, the staff took LaRicko back to the doctor to have his eyes tested again to find that his eyesight was back on track, so LaRicko did not have to wear glasses after all.

Chapter 8

God Showing Up and Showing Out!

*O*ctober 17 was the day that LaRicko was moved to his new room, which allowed him to be totally responsible for dressing himself, combing his hair, and brushing his teeth. I was concerned once again regarding LaRicko being advanced so soon to the next level because, as I had shared before, my son could hardly hold a spoon to his mouth because of his hands being contracted under at the wrist. And also, in the new area of promotion, LaRicko was also responsible for going to classes on a daily basis. The therapist would set up a list of LaRicko's classes on a board in a designated area, and he was responsible for following those instructions. That would allow the therapist to track LaRicko's progress also. So I was wondering to myself how in the world was my son going to manage with doing those things, *and he was also still in a wheelchair? But the upside was, the nurses would still come and help LaRicko take a shower, which was a blessing. The staff at the facility really pushed the patients there to a speedy recovery, which I felt was great, so I tried not to think so negatively regarding LaRicko being placed in a room where he would be responsible for himself. But I just continued to trust God! When I got up there on the weekend, we saw that LaRicko also had a roommate who was actually from St. Louis also. The young man appeared to be a very nice guy, and he was sharing with us how LaRicko would never come out of his room and spend time with the rest of the patients at recreation time. That was a level that my son just didn't feel comfortable with—mingling with the patients. LaRicko was such a loner at that time, but the young man said, "I will keep encouraging him to come and spend some time with the rest of us." There were lots of fun things that the facility would do for the patients, which included playing games, watching movies, and there were times that they would just gather together in the recreation room to just simply talk. The activities were being done to keep the patients from just sitting in their rooms alone. And LaRicko would do just the opposite, which was to stay in his room, but I felt that he needed a little more time before he would get comfortable enough to do those things.*

But overall, I was so happy to see LaRicko, in his wheelchair with his feet actually on the floor, pushing him-self around. I prayed that I would see the day that my son would get to that point. That allowed me to see that LaRicko's legs were getting stronger and stronger, so I began to think to myself that it wouldn't be very long before my son would be able to walk. We enjoyed another Blessed weekend.

Just when I thought all the mean and inconsiderate people had been weeded out of the facility, I found that there was still one around. When

I called my son to talk to him and to check and see how his day went, I found out that he was crying. I knew at that point of LaRicko's recovery that the last thing that his doctors and nurses wanted to hear was that LaRicko was upset and crying. So I began to ask my son what was bothering him, and he said the nurse that was assisting that night was being very mean to him. I asked my son in what way was the nurse being mean, and he shared with me how the nurse picked him up out of his wheelchair and threw him in the bed, and she began to talk really mean to him. And I asked my son what the nurse's name was so that I could call the front desk and inform them of what had gone on. LaRicko was a bit afraid to tell me her name because he thought she would come back and hurt him after I reported her to the front desk. As the conversation went on, my son finally told me her name, and it was ironic that her name was the same as mine. And I assured my son that when I would call the front desk and inform them of what was going on, I would ask them to assure me that the nurse wouldn't come back in his room so he wouldn't have to be afraid. Of course, I was livid! After I hung up the phone from my son, I called the front desk of the facility right away and spoke with one of the nurses to inform them of what was going on. As soon as I began to inform the nurse about what was going on, he said to me that the rest of the staff had noticed the nurse and that it would be her last night working for the facility. That nurse already was aware that she was no longer wanted at their facility, but they allowed her one more day to work, and she was harassing several of their patients. So to make my son and me feel better, the nurse that I spoke with at the front desk went into LaRicko's room and spoke with him while I was still on the phone to inform LaRicko that the particular nurse would not be back in his room anymore. It was still a bit hard for me to accept that such a cruel person was upsetting my son, but I prayed and trusted that God was working it out for us. I didn't want my son to begin to be too uncomfortable with trying to be responsible for him-self. We were trying to push them to get stronger, and issues such as that could have been a big setback for LaRicko.

As the week went on, I received a call from LaRicko's counselors to inform me that they would like for me to come to a conference that they were going to be having with LaRicko on that upcoming Friday. Of course, I could hardly wait to hear their thoughts regarding my son's recovery. So my son's fiancée and I went up there on that Friday to attend the conference to find out how well my son was doing. The counselors wanted to inform us on what had been going on with my son as well as wanting us to hear from LaRicko directly on what his goals were mentally and physically. When we arrived there for the meeting, the counselors took LaRicko's fiancée, a couple of nurses, and me into a conference room, and a few minutes later, they wheeled LaRicko in (he was in a wheelchair). As LaRicko sat across the table from us, the counselors began to ask him questions regarding what his goals were, and I was really impressed with LaRicko's answers. LaRicko said, first of all, that he wanted to be able to walk again so that he can get out of that wheelchair, and he included that he wanted to regain his strength so that he would be able to go back to work so that he could take care of his fiancée and future baby. And I thought that was a great conference because it allowed the patient to set their own goals, and they helped the patients succeed in their goals. Shortly after the conference, LaRicko's physical therapist allowed LaRicko's fiancée and me to go over to watch LaRicko for a little bit in his physical therapy class. I was almost with tears of joy when I saw the therapist help LaRicko on a treadmill, and LaRicko held on to the side rails as the therapist strapped a belt around LaRicko's waist and turned on the speed. As LaRicko began to walk on the treadmill, I couldn't help but notice that he was really working *hard on strengthening his legs. After LaRicko got off the treadmill, I noticed that his physical therapy instructor had placed a big wide belt around LaRicko's waist as well as his own, and then he lifted LaRicko up from the back of the belt and began walking with LaRicko down the hallway. Oh my goodness, I thought to myself. So those were the things that went on during the week in the classes. That's why LaRicko was always so much better each weekend that we would come up to visit. The therapist worked with the patients really hard during the week, which was awesome! So after the conference and the physical therapy classes for my son, the instructor helped LaRicko back into his wheelchair, and afterward, his fiancée and I decided that we were going to go over to get something to eat and proceed to the facility where we had to spend our nights while we were there. But before we left the hospital area, we had been informed that the staff had planned to take all the patients out to the movies the next day. Of course, LaRicko really didn't want to go, but we managed to talk him into it. I prayed that LaRicko would eventually get better by the kind of attitude that he had, which caused him to want to be isolated from people. I had hoped that the isolation attitude was stemmed from trying to come around out of his illness as well as maybe the medication was playing a role.*

Well, on that Saturday, which was movie day for the patients, we waited around for my son as he dressed himself; I was really impressed today on how much further he had come in his progressing. The nurse pushed LaRicko's wheelchair as my son's fiancée and I walked down the halls, heading to the bus that was waiting to take us to the movies. As I was walking, my cell phone began to ring. It was a call from LaRicko's favorite aunt and uncle, who were also better known as LaRicko's second mother and father, from Arkansas, to inform me that they were on their way to Mount Vernon to surprise LaRicko. I was so happy because I knew that LaRicko was going to be so surprised as well as happy. So I was looking forward to a whole day of excitement because I could hardly wait to see how my son was going to react during his first time out in the public after being closed up for so long. We stood back as the nurses began to place my son's wheelchair onto the lifter of the bus to head for the movies. I just couldn't believe how outstanding things were at that facility. I'll never forget how LaRicko began to look around at the guy that was holding the back of his wheelchair as the lifter was raised, as if to say, "Please don't let me go," but I knew that LaRicko was in good hands with that guy. That particular person always took very good care of LaRicko. So as we boarded the bus, the nurse began to talk to the patients and tease them just to make the bus ride a fun trip, and it was just that!

When we got the patients to the movies, I had never seen so many nice people in one place. We actually received first-class service from start to finish of the visit. I felt that we were so blessed. My son was sitting there in his wheelchair, staring at the crowd. I didn't know if he was really into the movie or not, but I knew he did appear to have been watching the crowd. And as the time went on, I was impressed at how well LaRicko had done in the public that day. Thank God!

When we returned back to the facility, I phoned LaRicko's aunt and uncle from Mariana, Arkansas, to inform them that we were on our way back upstairs with LaRicko; they were waiting there in his room. I could hardly wait to see LaRicko's face. So as we got off the elevator pushing my son's wheelchair, his fiancée and I began smiling as we were walking behind him, and when we turned the corner and pushed LaRicko into his room, there stood his aunt Doris and uncle Bill. LaRicko didn't know what to say. His reactions were still a bit slow, but at the same time, you could tell he was very happy. LaRicko's aunt Doris sat there with him as a mother would and talked and laughed with him as well. She shared with LaRicko how proud she was of his progress. Doris was such a loving and caring person that I was so glad that she was there. LaRicko's uncle Bill lay in LaRicko's bed and told him that Uncle Bill needed that bed to rest in; it was time for LaRicko to stay up as Uncle Bill relaxed. How funny! His uncle Bill had been such a wonderful uncle to LaRicko. So as that evening continued, we sat in LaRicko's room and had a wonderful family gathering. We took pictures and just enjoyed each other. That was another blessed weekend.

We were headed for another week, praying that things continued to get better and better. I called LaRicko to see how his day went, and he said things were going good. I would always call during the day as well to speak with the nurses to find out if LaRicko's spirits were still looking up and to see how well he had done in the mornings getting dressed. LaRicko was also responsible for going to the board that was conveniently placed in the halls for the patients and pointing out his name and find out the classes that he was going to be taking that day. The nurse would inform me how well LaRicko had done or if he had a hard time finding his way that day. I thought that the information board was a great tool for the patients. It was a large blackboard that was in the hallway, and all the patients that were at that level of rehabilitation would have to go to that board by a certain time in the morning and write down their classes for the day and the room numbers of the classes and the time that they were to be in class, and that was the beginning of preparing them for the outside world. It was still a bit difficult for LaRicko to remember his schedule, but he was at least trying very hard, and I, as well as the counselors, was impressed with LaRicko trying at that point.

On the twenty-eighth day of October, which is my mother's birthday, I decided to call to check and see how LaRicko was doing, which was my usual, and of course, the staff knew me personally. When I spoke to the nurse and asked how my son was doing that day, the nurse said to me, "He is doing great! The last time I saw him, he was walking down the hall toward his room." My mouth flew open; I asked, "Walking?" The nurse said, "Yes, they took LaRicko's wheelchair from him today." She included that normally, their patients would have to graduate from a wheelchair to a walker, from the walker to a cane, then from there, the patients were allowed after a while to walk on their own, but the staff was so impressed that LaRicko went from the wheelchair to walking on his own. I turned around in the office and shared the news with the rest of the office; everyone in the office was just as stunned as I was about LaRicko walking so soon. One of the ladies on the job turned and said to me that she couldn't believe that my son was still alive. She included that she just knew that LaRicko was going to die. And all I could say was ***"God showed up and showed out!"***

Chapter 9

We've come This Far by Faith

I called LaRicko later that evening *to see how things were going with him, and he was so excited to share with me that he was walking. He said, "I'm doing real well, Mom." He added that as he was walking down the hall earlier, he had lost his balance and fell in the hallway a few steps from his room and that he was worried that the doctor would give him the wheelchair back. And I told LaRicko that the doctor wouldn't dare to have done anything such as that because they wanted him to continue to move forward on his recovery. I explained to my son that the staff was aware that his legs were still very weak. He said, "Mom, when I fell, I couldn't get back up right at the moment, so I just slid down the hall until I got to my room and went in." I encouraged LaRicko by telling him that he was doing great; I just wanted him to keep up the good work as long as he was not hurting himself in the process. I said to him, "Just continue to work at getting stronger and stronger." We all were so ecstatic about the fact that LaRicko was walking. I thank God for giving me the faith and strength to hold on. It was truly a miracle!*

So as the next week went on, of course I did my usual calling to check on my son. And I found out that on the thirty-first of October, which was Halloween, the facility had given a barbecue for the patients. They were all sitting around outside, enjoying the different entertainments, and as the nurses began to serve the patients, everyone was so impressed with my son because LaRicko helped serve the patients who were still in a wheelchair and could not walk. The nurse shared with me that LaRicko would go over and get the patients' food for them. The nurse also included that my son helped clean up the area after the barbecue and assisted them as they prepared for the hayride that the patients were going to be taking afterward. That was really a wonderful time for my son because LaRicko was actually spending time with others whereas he'd normally sit in his room and not come out to visit. So LaRicko had begun to show a lot more alertness.

When I came back to visit LaRicko for the weekend, which was the first time for me to see him walking on his own, I was like a mother who was watching her baby take his first footsteps. I walked into my son's room, and he was still in the bed awaiting our arrival because he knew that we would show up every weekend and bring him breakfast. When LaRicko looked up and saw us walk into his room, he began to get out of bed. We were just waiting for him to walk, which was so exciting for us. When he got up to walk over to the bathroom to wash his face, we watched him as he was walking. He made steps as a baby would, weak and as if he could lose his balance at any time, but I was so thankful to the Lord for the baby steps because I knew as time went on, LaRicko would get stronger and stronger.

I can do all things through Christ which strengtheneth me. (Philippians 4:13)

As LaRicko walked to the bathroom, we were letting LaRicko know how proud we were of him that he was doing so well. That really encouraged him to work even harder. After he came out of the bathroom, he began to eat his breakfast, and I sat there beside him as he shared with me all the things that he had gone through in class in the past week. LaRicko finished his breakfast and proceeded to make his bed. "Wow!" I said. "You are really showing out!" He just blushed as he continued to pull up the covers on the bed. I began to take pictures as he straightened his room and got his clothes out for the day and laid them out on the bed, and then he proceeded to go to the bathroom to take his shower. I could hardly believe my eyes. It was amazing how well he was doing with his hands, being that they were still contracted at the wrist, but he was working so well even though that was the case. We truly had a great weekend!

As the day went on, we took LaRicko outside so that he could walk around and enjoy the outside. He was so proud of how well he was coming around also. We began to walk around the facility, and all of a sudden, there was a group of nurses standing outside taking a break, and they began to shout out LaRicko's name. One of them said, "LaRicko, is that you?" As he stood there staring at them as if he was trying to figure out how they knew his name, he said, "Yes, it's me." All those nurses ran over and gathered around LaRicko and began to hug him and remind him of how far he had come since he had been there at the facility. The nurses were so happy and impressed. They included that LaRicko was recovering so fast, being that he was in such a bad condition when he first got there; it was unbelievable. I began to thank God even more for having favor in us.

Thou hast granted me life and favour, and thy visitation hath preserved my spirit. (Job 10:12)

We began to take pictures of my son and the nurses as they continued to love on him and encourage him to keep up the good work.

As that weekend went on, we sat in LaRicko's room; I would notice how the nurses would come in my son's room and ask him what day was it, and he would try hard to remember what day it was, and then the nurse would begin to administer LaRicko's medication to him, and before they would give him his medication, the nurse would ask him to name the medicine that he was going to be taking at the time, and they would also ask LaRicko how many times of the day did he take that type of medicine. That was a really difficult task for him at the time, but there was yet a great test for him because the staff was only trying to prepare LaRicko for the challenges that he was going to have to deal with in the outside world. I would watch my son's facial expressions as he would look as if he was trying so hard to remember the names of his meds and the days of the week; he was really trying hard. Each time a nurse would walk into LaRicko's room, no matter how many times a day, they would ask him the same questions to make sure that he would continue to focus on those things. They had already informed LaRicko that he would need to know all those things prior to leaving the facility, so he would really try hard. I remember that my son had a calendar in *his room on the wall, and as each day would pass, he would mark a line through that day so that he could keep up with the days of the week, which was a great idea. But he was really struggling with the names of his medication, but that was okay with me because he was still alive, and I thanked God for the miracle!*

As time went on, LaRicko began to get a little stronger as the weeks passed. We knew that his recovery was going to be taken one day at a time, and of course, we were not going to rush anything, but we were just thanking and trusting God for all the baby steps.

Around the first part of November, LaRicko was at a point where he was going to be receiving a badge for each time he completed a class. The badges were different colors. The colors of the badges indicated how far you were responsible to go on your own without any assistance. At that point, LaRicko had earned a cream-colored badge, which allowed him to be able to go off the premises with us when we would come up on the weekends to visit with him. Where everything was getting better and better for him, it allowed him to go and see a little more of the town of Mount Vernon.

So our first visit off the premises with LaRicko consisted of a trip to the zoo in the Springfield area. LaRicko got dressed and finished up with breakfast, and as soon as we got our pass to take him out for the day, we left and headed for the zoo. Needless to say, I was a bit concerned about taking LaRicko too far away from the facility because I didn't know if he was ready for the outside world as of yet with walking around. But when we arrived at the zoo and began to get out of the car, LaRicko proceeded to get out, and because we were parked on an incline and he was still pretty weak, he lost his balance and began to fall. I ran and got behind him so that he could fall on me, and as we went down to the ground, I didn't feel the impact at all because I was focused on protecting my son from any injuries. Once we got up off the ground, I watched him as he began to break out into such a sweat as he appeared to be so nervous. I kept encouraging him that it was only normal for him to have lost his balance, being that we weren't aware that we were on an incline and he was still a bit weak. "Stop worrying about it. You are okay," I said. And at the same time, I was praying, "Lord, strengthen him in his weakness."

And he said unto me, My grace is sufficient for thee: for my strength is made perfect in weakness. Most gladly therefore will I rather glory in my infirmities, that the power of Christ may rest upon me. (2 Corinthians 12:9)

We began to walk up to enter the gates to head into the zoo, but I noticed that LaRicko really didn't look well enough at that point to take advantage of the visit into the zoo. We sat him down right at the gate so that he could calm down and collect his energy. While LaRicko was sitting there trying to feel better, he asked me, "Mom, are you going to tell the nurse that I fell?" And I shared with him that if I did, it would only be to help him because they really wanted to know if there was an area in LaRicko's recovery that was needed to be focused on more than others. But my son was convinced that it would prolong his stay at the facility if I shared it with the nurses. I had to pray and put that situation in God's hand as always because I knew LaRicko was worried and was very nervous about not being able to leave the premises anymore for a while as well. After sitting there in the area for a little while, we decided to get ready to go back to the facility. On the way back, we stopped and ate at one of my favorite chicken places, and while we were there, I noticed that my son appeared to be really sad, so I asked him, "What's wrong?" He said, "Mom, please don't tell the nurse I fell, they are not going to let me leave anymore." I convinced him that I'd keep that between me, his dad, fiancée, and him. For some reason, that really was disturbing to my son, and I didn't want him to continue to stress himself out about anything.

So when we got back to the facility, the staff began to ask LaRicko to tell them about his visit away from the facility and they also wanted him to share with them where he went. That was a test to see if he would remember all the things that he done throughout the time spent out. But overall, it ended up being another blessed weekend with LaRicko.

The next weekend in November, we had another opportunity to take LaRicko off the premises of the facility, wherein we decided to go to breakfast at a McDonalds in Springfield, and he enjoyed that very well. Afterward, we decided to go to Walmart to see how much energy LaRicko had to walk around. And as the shopping time passed, my son did great! He even showed me how well he remembered how to pick out his clothes. I thought it was kind of funny at that point because I could always pick his clothes when he was a little boy, but as he had grown older, my taste for his clothes was not suffice. And as long as he was in a coma, of course he didn't realize the clothes that I had picked for him. Being that he had become aware of those clothes that he was wearing, he began to pick out different-looking clothes. How funny! It was interesting to me how our life was repeating itself. But I did notice that when he saw the T-shirt that had the twenty-third psalm on it, he was so excited about it, and he just had to have it. So after shopping, we proceeded to head back to the facility because we had to have LaRicko back at a certain time. We were being tested as well. The nurse also gave me a checklist, which was used to let the staff know how well my son performed on different things as well as how he reacted at different places. And I felt that he did great on his second visit off the premises after learning how to walk. LaRicko never complained about being tired or anything. With LaRicko not complaining about anything was another blessing that we didn't have to concern ourselves with, him getting too tired or out of breath.

The whole weekend was really great because the next day after LaRicko got out of bed and got him-self dressed, we went out and got breakfast, and then we decided to spend time with LaRicko at one of their local parks. It was really nice how we sat around and watched the ducks in the water and took pictures of our whole outing, and one thing I saw that was really nice and reminded me a lot of myself was a mother duck who was so overly protective of her babies that she made sure we did not come too close to them. She looked as if she wanted to attack us, and I understood totally how she felt in protecting her child because that was exactly what I had been doing so strongly for the past few months.

Well, we were at the point that LaRicko was performing so much better physically, but mentally, his memory was one of their main focal points because he was having issues remembering the names of his medication as well as the times that he was supposed to take them. The nurses in the past would come into the room and bring him his medication, but not at that stage of his progress. The nurses wanted LaRicko to come up to the front desk and request his meds at the times that was he supposed to take them. That was also testing his memory. One of the staff would come and stand in front of the calendar that was in LaRicko's room and ask him what day was it and what was the date, and my son always had an issue remembering that. He struggled at times and would get it right, and there were other times that he would just do the guessing thing. This was not good enough.

Now that my son had gotten to the point that he was able to walk and he was attending his classes each day, he had begun to concern himself with when was he going to be able to go home. He hadn't completed all his goals that he had set for himself, but he was ready to go home. LaRicko's hands were still contracted under at the wrist, but the physical therapist was still working on my son's hands each day in physical therapy classes. LaRicko was also attending speech therapy and several other classes that were preparing him to go home, but he really wanted to hear a confirmed date.

So as the week went on I spoke with one of the counselors and I was informed that LaRicko may be able to go home on the eleventh of November. We were all happy to hear that, but the counselor also reminded me that LaRicko still needed to continue with further classes because they could see that he was not really ready for the outside world without more therapy classes. So I spoke with LaRicko to let him know what I was told, and he began to get excited. So I told my son that he was going to have to work even harder mentally as well as physically because I had noticed how weak he still was. But I knew that it would get better at God's timing.

After the week passed, the counselor sent me a letter to inform me that LaRicko's doctor felt that he needed to stay a while longer at the facility because he was not ready to go home at that point, which was very disappointing. When I called LaRicko on November 11 to talk to *him, he was crying very hard because he was looking so forward to going home. I was sad for him, but it was at a point that all I could do was pray for my son to understand, and he kept saying to me, "Mom, I don't understand why I have to stay longer."*

> **Trust in the Lord with all thine heart; and lean not unto thine own understanding. In all thy ways acknowledge him, and he shall direct thy paths. (Proverbs 3:5-6)**

So after we went up the following weekend to visit him, my son was pretty down in the dumps. His father looked at me as we walked into his room and pointed at the calendar that LaRicko had on his wall. I was a bit saddened when I noticed that the promised date for LaRicko to leave there was the eleventh of November. I could tell how upset my son was on that day because he had taken a pen and blackened that date out on the calendar to the point that he had rubbed a hole in that area.

I looked at him as he sat on his bed with a sad face, and I reminded him that the doctors and nurses were only trying to help him, which I felt was a really good thing. But of course, LaRicko didn't look at things that way. He just wanted to leave. I sat down beside him and hugged him and began to explain to him that we didn't want to rush getting out of there, and he may relapse and have to come back. "Would you want that to happen?" I asked, and he said no, so I suggested to my son for us to just take one day at a time because he was going to be going home real soon. So after that smooth over happened, we began to prepare to go outside and enjoy the day. We walked around the facility and showed LaRicko our rooms that were across the way from the facility where he was residing because he hadn't been in that area. He was getting better as the day went on. We took LaRicko down to an area truck stop to eat a buffet dinner, which was really nice. He enjoyed that as well. Each evening, we would sit with LaRicko in his room until it was time for us to leave so that he could go to bed, and before we left, I would see to it that he had his bath and was ready for bed.

On the next morning, we spent the usual time with LaRicko and took him up to the store where he wanted to purchase some items before we left to head back to St. Louis for the week. Then we came back to the facility and proceeded to spend quality time with LaRicko before we headed home. The visits were getting better and better just to have known that LaRicko was walking and talking on his own. I thank you, Lord, for it all.

O Give thanks unto the Lord; for he is good: for his mercy endureth for ever. (Psalm 136:1)

What was even better about the day, not only did LaRicko remember the time that he was to take his medication, but he actually asked for his meds by name. He was really trying hard to go home. Awesome!

So as the week went on, I received a call from the counselor of the facility, and she shared with me that the doctors, nurses, and the other counselors had a discussion regarding LaRicko, and they all felt that he was doing really well. They all still had concerns regarding LaRicko in certain areas of his recovery, but for the most part, they all felt that he was doing great. The counselor included that the group would love to keep LaRicko for a couple more months to get him to a much better level. But my son appeared to be getting a bit depressed because he was ready to go home, and the counselor told to me that they never want to see a patient fall into depression because it would make the recovery period even more difficult for them. So before they would allow that situation to happen, they would simply allow the patient to go home and order outpatient therapy treatments with a facility closer to where the patient lived. And of course, I thought that was very supportive of the staff to allow those options for LaRicko. The counselor also wanted to know what our plans were for the Thanksgiving holiday, which was coming up the following week. I replied, "We're going to come up and spend that time with LaRicko." The counselor asked what had we normally done for the Thanksgiving holiday, and I said that we normally went down to Arkansas to spend that time with the family, but under those circumstances, we were just going to visit with LaRicko in Mount Vernon. The counselor said to me that she was going to talk to the doctors and the other counselors and see if LaRicko could go home for the day so that he could be with the family. I reminded her that Arkansas was hours away from Mount Vernon. It would be difficult for us to drive there and back in one day. The counselor informed me that the patients were only allowed to be checked out of the facility only for one weekend during their entire stay, which was usually the holiday. And they really didn't want us to have to sit at the rehabilitation center on the holiday. But I was okay with it because I wanted to be with my son, even if it meant to sit there all weekend. I was concerned about how LaRicko would feel about going home if need be anyway, being that I hadn't discussed that with him.

So I called LaRicko later that afternoon to see how he was doing and he appeared to still be in a downbeat mode because he felt that he was ready to come home. While talking to LaRicko on the phone, I asked, "What do you think about coming home for Thanksgiving?" And he asked, "Just for a day?" And I said, "Yes, but at least you can get *some time away from the facility." With disappointment in his voice, he said, "I would rather just stay here. I don't want to be teased with going home and having to come back here. I'll just stay here," he said. Then I began to pray that LaRicko would have a change of heart about the offer because I thought that the counselors and the doctors wanted to see how well LaRicko was going to react away from the facility as well. So I said to him, "Just think of all the people that are going to be happy to see you." Well, that didn't go over too well either. After a while of trying to convince LaRicko to want to go home on the holiday, I said to him whatever he wanted to do on Thanksgiving was what we were going to do. LaRicko was okay with that thought.*

The very next day, the counselor called me on the phone again to inform me that the doctor had decided to allow LaRicko that entire Thanksgiving holiday weekend to go home with us to Arkansas. They were going to release LaRicko on Wednesday, which was the day before Thanksgiving, so that he could go to Arkansas, and we didn't have to bring him back until the Sunday after the holiday. The counselor was so surprised at the decision that the doctor had allowed us because that had never happened before (regarding a four-day vacation from the facility). The longest time that had been given to a patient on leave from the facility was a weekend. I knew that the Lord granted us favor on that decision. I was excited when she shared that information with me. I could hardly wait to talk to LaRicko again regarding his decision, to share with him that he was allowed by the doctor to actually go to Arkansas and spend the entire time with the family on Thanksgiving. I reminded myself that in my prayers a couple months back, I claimed through faith that my son will be able to slice the turkey for us on Thanksgiving, which I had shared that statement with several people in my life, and we were going to have that opportunity.

Then touched he their eyes, saying, According to your faith be it unto you. (Matthew 9:29)

Thank you, Lord. And at that point, I also felt that my son obviously was doing pretty good that the doctor felt comfortable enough to allow us to take him for so long from the facility for such a far distance away.

That weekend was going to be an exciting weekend to me because I was going to share with LaRicko what the doctor was going to allow us to do once I got to his room to visit with him. After I got there and walked into my son's room, he looked really well. He had been moved to his own private room, which was really nice. I sat down beside him, and I said, "Guess what." He asked, "What?" I began to share with him that the doctor was going to allow him to leave the facility on Wednesday and that he didn't have to return back until the following Sunday. I asked LaRicko, "How do you feel about that decision?" He was still a bit back and forth about the idea. But I told him that all the family was looking forward to seeing him. I continued with so many of the family members had called from out of town, and they were going to meet us in Arkansas to see him. But for some reason, LaRicko was still a bit reluctant about the idea. I said to him, "Just let me know what you prefer to do before I leave and head back home from the weekend." I needed to let the doctor know what decision we were going make so that the doctor could prepare the documents to have my son released for the weekend as well as have all the medications ready for LaRicko before we left. And as that weekend continued, LaRicko decided that it may actually be a good idea. He was at least willing to try. I was happy with his change of heart.

As the weekend ended, we informed LaRicko that we would be back in three days to pick him up for a trip to Arkansas. He had begun to mark his calendar so that he would remember when the day was coming up.

After I got home from visiting with LaRicko, I began to get bombarded with phone calls from family members to find out if LaRicko was really going to be able to make it to Arkansas for Thanksgiving. I was so proud to share with the family members that what they had heard regarding LaRicko coming home for Thanksgiving was true. We were so looking forward to the holiday. All of LaRicko's aunts, uncles, cousins, and grandparents were ecstatic to hear that. They all were going to be traveling to Arkansas from Michigan, Chicago, West Memphis, Memphis, and other places to see LaRicko. It was beginning to feel like a family reunion. God has really been blessing us with so much support from so many loved ones. When I shared that LaRicko was going to Arkansas for Thanksgiving with the people on my job, they were just speechless. They couldn't believe that he was recovering so soon. Once again, God has shown up and is showing out!

At the time, I was planning to rent an SUV so that my son could have a comfortable ride to travel to Arkansas, being that it was a long trip. The car that I had was not going to allow LaRicko to lie down in the backseat, and I knew that he would need to stretch out and relax after a while during the trip, being that it was so far. As I began to check out car rental places to get an SUV, my best friend called and asked me what day we were planning to leave to head to Arkansas. I told her, and she said, "I will be bringing my SUV over so that LaRicko would have room enough to relax." I thanked God for her because she was always there *for us. And for her to allow me to use her SUV through the holiday was such a blessing.*

We left early Wednesday morning, which was Thanksgiving eve, to go up and pick LaRicko up for the trip, and when we got there, I didn't know if he had changed his mind again because he had been back and forth with his decision, but to my surprise, when I walked into my son's room, he had his clothes laid out to be placed in his suitcase. I asked, "Are you ready to go?" LaRicko said with a smile on his face, "I'm looking forward to seeing the family, and I hope they're anxious to see me." I assured him that they were excited also. Being that his hair had grown so much, I had begun to braid it every weekend to keep my son from having to concern himself with it, so prior to us leaving the facility, we had to wait on his medication to be delivered to him. I decided to braid his hair before we got on the road. And as I was standing there braiding LaRicko's hair, his phone rang, and I was surprised by that because my son was normally in class at that time, but the instructors allowed LaRicko to miss class that day so that we could get on the road earlier to head out of town. And when my son answered the phone, to his surprise, it was our pastor on the other line. My son was so excited because through the whole time that he had been talking, he had been asking me to have the pastor call him because he wanted to ask the pastor to pray for him, and I would always tell LaRicko that the pastor was going to call him. So when LaRicko actually got the phone call from our Pastor, he thanked the pastor for praying for him, and he shared with our pastor that he was going to be leaving for Arkansas for the entire Thanksgiving weekend, and the pastor gave him his blessings. That phone call made my son's day. He said, "Wow, Mom, the holiday is starting to be great already." He had always thought so highly of our pastor, so that phone call meant an awful lot to LaRicko.

After we got everything that LaRicko needed for the trip, we proceeded to the lobby where several of the staff members were waiting to give us hugs and their blessing for the holiday season. They were happy and sad at the same time. They shared with LaRicko how much they were going to miss him. But they wanted him to spend time with the family. So as we left the facility, I still had a little nervousness in my spirit only because I hadn't spent a whole day with LaRicko away from the facility. I prayed to the Lord that it would be a blessed trip and that my son would be okay through all the cold weather, as well as keeping LaRicko's strength up for the long drive because my son was still very, very weak. I would watch LaRicko's feet all the time as he would walk because most of the time, it appeared that he could hardly lift them up, so I would always stand close to my son to assure that if he fell, he would land on me. So as we traveled down the long roads, I would look back at my son and make sure he was comfortable. I would ask him, "Are you okay?" and he would answer me with his weak voice, "Yes, Mom." After traveling for so long, the cell phones began to ring from several different family members wanting to know how much longer it was going to be before we got there. It was so nice because everybody was so excited, which made LaRicko feel so special. He really didn't realize how happy the family was that he was recovering.

After hours and hours on the road, we finally made it to my parents' house. When we got there, my dad greeted us at the door; we hugged, and he hugged LaRicko and told him how happy he was to see him. LaRicko said, "Granddaddy, I'm glad to see you too." LaRicko had begun to tear up a little bit. So LaRicko's dad walked with him into the den where LaRicko sat on the couch. My mom was in the bed relaxing, and I walked back to wake her to let her know we were there, and Mom jumped up with excitement; she said hello to me, gave me a hug, and walked straight to the den where LaRicko was sitting, and she said, "Hi, Ricko, get up and let Grandma see you walk." So my son struggled from the couch with his weak legs and walked over to his grandmother, and she had such a proud smile on her face. She said, "God is good," and I agreed, "Yes, he is."

When it came time for me to give my son his medication, I discovered that the facility did not give him enough of the medication that he needed. I had to call the facility so that they could call the pharmacy in Arkansas to forward a prescription for LaRicko. I thought to myself how the enemy was trying to interrupt the blessed trip, but God had a ram in the bush for us. We had to go to another pharmacy to get the medication, which they informed us that didn't normally carry the medication, but they actually had it at the time. God had shown up once again.

As we began to relax for the evening, being that it was my first night away from the facility with LaRicko, I continued to be the overprotective and concerned mother, so I made sure that I slept on the same bed that my son slept. I told LaRicko that if he needed to get up and go to the bathroom or anything throughout the night, he needed to make sure that he would wake me so that I could go with him. I did not want to take any chances of my son falling or anything, being that he was still very, very weak. The first night actually went very well. Praise the Lord!

When we got up out of bed the next morning, I prepared LaRicko's clothes for the day and thanked God for allowing my son and me to see another blessed Thanksgiving Day together. As I began to run my son's bathwater, he was receiving several phone calls from so many loved ones, which was making him feel better about taking the trip.

Just when I thought the bathing of my son was over, here I was bathing him as if he was a newborn because he was so weak. And he was twenty-six years old. I'll never forget how I had to stand behind him in the tub in order to lift him up and down because he didn't have the strength to do it on his own as of yet, but I thanked God for him being there. I was such a proud mother at that point; it did not matter to me what I needed to do to care for my son. (We just never know what types of hands we are going to be dealt in life.) After the bath, I got LaRicko dressed and proceeded to the kitchen where his grandma (my mother) had prepared breakfast for us. When we got in the kitchen, we had several family members there to see LaRicko early. My son was very happy to see the love that was shown to him.

As the afternoon went on, Mom finished preparing the Thanksgiving dinner, and we all gathered around the table as my mother began to bless the food and thank God for the miracle that we had been blessed with. Things began to happen as I claimed it to happen a few months back, which was my son slicing the Thanksgiving turkey. It was such as blessing to all of us. After we had dinner, the house began to flood with all kinds of houseguests, family members, and friends, and I was so happy because LaRicko really wasn't aware of how much everybody wanted to see him until that day.

LaRicko's Cousin Dennis came and surprised him with a much-needed coat; my son was so happy and excited about that. My son's cousin Geneva brought him some Timberland boots that LaRicko just fell in love with, and other family members and friends just showered him with gifts and so much love. LaRicko's cousins cuddled him and made it no secret of how happy they were to have him back. I'll never forget when his cousin Nikki walked in and looked at LaRicko.

She began to hug him and lie all over him as she asked him with her hands on her hip, "Now, Ricko, what was that stunt you pulled?" as she began to giggle. It was very cute as well as funny, but I thought, That was a stunt that only God could have pulled him out of, and praises to the Lord that he did!

As the evening went on and while we just enjoyed all the company that was there, the young man that I spoke with on the phone on the ninth of September, who prayed for my son at that time when LaRicko was in the worst condition, called. The young man was Prophet Michael; he had told me way back in September to put my hands on my son's legs as he prayed for him. He spoke over LaRicko's healing back then. Prophet said to me that my son was going to shock the doctors and nurses at that hospital because he was going to walk back into that hospital and show them that God is a miracle worker. When Prophet Michael called and said that he was on his way to see my son, I could hardly wait to see that young man. When Prophet Michael knocked at the door, I opened it and let him in; I hugged him, and right away, he began to minister to me, sharing with me what the spirit of the Lord had shown him to share with me. I remember so well the statement that he made to me. He said, "Sister Diane, thank you for not giving your son to the devil. I thank God for your strong faith in God." I was enjoying every minute of what Prophet Michael had to say. Then as he walked through the house, he would stop and minister to some of the other family members in the house that he was led by the spirit to minister to. Prophet Michael had certain people at the house in tears because he was sharing different things that the Lord was putting in his spirit about them that they hadn't even spoken with the young man before. Everyone had begun to focus on the prophet because he was such an anointed young man. But the best was yet to come. Prophet Michael finally made it to the den where LaRicko was sitting. He walked to the door, and as several different ones were sitting around, the prophet said, "Don't point LaRicko out. I'm going to walk straight to him." And the young man did just that. He sat down beside my son and began to minister to him. I remember my son sitting there looking so serious, looking straight at Prophet Michael as he was talking, as if he was just taking it all in. A few times I noticed that my son had begun to shed some tears, but I could tell that the tears were tears of joy. He shared with LaRicko the things that the Lord had placed in his spirit to share with him. And as he sat there talking to my son, Prophet looked up at me as well and said, "The things that God has placed in our lives for us to do, don't fight against them. You need to do what God has for you both to do." I will never forget what that young man said to me. He said, "Please don't fight against what God has for you to do." He included that it would be the worst thing that you could do if you would try and fight against what God has for you to do. And I have always kept that in my mind, pondering about that constantly. Because I truly want to do what God has for me to do; it was my daily prayer for the Lord to order steps in his Word.

So as the evening went on, my son was so happy with that whole day. I knew that LaRicko was very happy that he decided to come and make the trip. We took all kinds of pictures as different people continued to come over and spend time with LaRicko. That was such a blessed Thanksgiving Day in November 2003!

As the rest of the weekend went on, my son just kept getting more and more company, and to look at him, you could see that he was beginning to feel so special. And I could not thank the friends and family enough for the support that they had given to us. I thank God for such a loving and blessed family.

And I will bless them that bless thee, and curse him that curseth thee: and in thee shall all families of the earth be blessed. (Genesis 12:3)

Well, the time had come for us to head back to St. Louis so that LaRicko could spend a moment with his fiancée and her family before he had to head back to Mount Vernon. So we left Arkansas on that Saturday morning, and we made it to St. Louis that evening, which was so cold, and it was sleeting outside as well. I remember being reluctant to allow my son to go visiting with his fiancée and her family because he appeared to be getting weaker and weaker, but he wanted to go so bad that I just prayed and put all things in the Lord's hands because I didn't want to appear to be selfish, but I could see that he could hardly walk because he had already overexerted himself with the company down in Arkansas, plus such a long ride from Mount Vernon there, and then the ride back to St. Louis didn't help matters either.

So as we got to St. Louis, I spoke with LaRicko's fiancée to make her aware of his condition, and she assured me that they had enough help at her family's house that would be happy to assist my son through the entire visit. And sure enough, when we drove up in front of LaRicko's fiancée's parents' house, his fiancée's uncles came out to help LaRicko walk into the house. I began feeling like a mother who was dropping her child off at school for the very first time, but I had to remind myself that LaRicko's fiancée's family loved him also and that they would take care of my son too. After they made it in the house with LaRicko, I hugged him as he sat there in the kitchen of their house looking so weak, and I said to him, "I love you, and call me when you're ready to come home." I walked out of their house. I was trying not to look back to show how concerned I really was, but I had to trust God that my son would be okay.

As the evening went on, I came home and tried to relax before I began to prepare for another long drive to take my son back to Mount Vernon the next day. And in the midst of all that, I began to thank God for blessing us with such a blessed trip to Arkansas and back to St. Louis and all the loving people that were communicating with us the entire trip. So after a while, I called over to his fiancée to check on LaRicko, and through the conversation, we decided not to bring LaRicko back out in the bad weather, so my son spent the entire night at his fiancée's house. And she said that he did very well throughout the night.

When I got up the very next morning, I prepared myself for another long trip and went over to his fiancée's parents' house to prepare my son for the trip as well. After getting everything together for the trip, LaRicko's dad came over to pick us up, and as we rode through the neighborhood, we went by the radio announcer's house who had been broadcasting LaRicko's name on the radio, requesting prayer through the whole time of LaRicko's illness. The radio announcer knew that the doctors had diagnosed that LaRicko was going to be a vegetable for the rest of his life. When the announcer walked out to our car and saw LaRicko, he could not believe his eyes; he was so excited and thanked us for bringing LaRicko over to see him. I also thanked the announcer for requesting prayers from the radio audience for LaRicko. I knew that when prayers go up, blessings come down, and here was a true sign of that. Then we drove around the corner and called a neighbor that lived across the street from us that was naming and claiming with me that my son was going to be fine. My neighbor said to me that when I was standing in my son's hospital room and I said to her, "Rosie, my baby is going to be fine," she said if I felt that way, she felt that way with me. So when my neighbor and her husband came outside to see LaRicko, they were so happy for us to see that LaRicko was doing great. I shared with them that he was only out of the facility for the holiday weekend, and we had to have him back in Mount Vernon by that afternoon and to pray for us for a blessed trip back, and my neighbors told LaRicko that they would be waiting on him to come home soon. My son had such big smile on his face.

On the way back to Mount Vernon, as we were riding down the highway, my son said, "Mom." I turned around in the car and looked back at him and his fiancée. LaRicko said, "I'm so glad that I went down to Arkansas to see the family." He added that the family showed him so much love. I was happy to hear LaRicko say that, being that he didn't feel that the trip was a good idea at first.

Once we got back to the facility and began to gather all of LaRicko's things out of the car, I asked LaRicko, "Are you glad to be back?" He answered, "Kind of," so that he could begin working toward the last few days that he had to spend there at the facility and so that he could come home for good. As we walked into the facility, everyone was so happy to see my son. They all began to call LaRicko's name out of excitement. They asked LaRicko to tell them all about his weekend. He was just smiling as he began to tell them all about his trip. Of course, LaRicko wore his new coat and shoes back to the facility, and the staff were complimenting him on his new attire. One of the staff members asked my son for his new shoes, and LaRicko just chuckled as if to say no way. LaRicko just smiled so big, being that he was so proud of all his new things. After a few minutes, one of the nurses weighed LaRicko, and she didn't appear to be too happy about the weight that he had gained. She said to me that we were going to need to slow down on allowing my son to eat as much because LaRicko didn't need too much weight on him at the point that he was in. I will never forget how serious the nurse looked at me. So at that point, I was going to make sure that my son didn't eat too much from that time on because the last thing that I wanted was for LaRicko to have some kind of setback in his recovery.

As I walked into LaRicko's room, he, his fiancée and his dad were sitting down relaxing for a minute after putting all of LaRicko's things away. I couldn't help but notice that my son was lying across his bed as if to say it was time for us to leave and go home. I really felt that LaRicko couldn't wait to get back to facility to get some rest because he was so tired from the long ride and all the company that he had enjoyed, and being that he was back at the facility, he wanted to work on getting some rest so that he could get his strength back. I knew that LaRicko had really enjoyed himself, but I also noticed that his energy level was getting pretty low, but overall, he was doing well. After spending a few minutes with my son in Mount Vernon, we decided to get back on the highway and head back home because we had to prepare for work the next day. LaRicko hugged us and said he loved us and that he would see us on the weekend. As I left my son, I felt so blessed about the entire weekend, and I just waited on the doctors to give me a call with the date for my son to be released from the facility for good.

As we traveled back to St. Louis, we had begun to discuss what our thoughts were regarding LaRicko's visit. We all thought he did very well being that it was his first visit out, and his fiancée and I agreed as we chuckled about the fact that he appeared to be happy about getting back to the facility because we tired him out, and he knew that he could at least get a good night's sleep without company interrupting.

When I spoke with LaRicko the next day, I asked him how he was doing, and he said he did really well in his classes. His physical therapist and speech therapist were really pleased with him that day. He said everyone was complimenting him on his new shoes. The staff even teased LaRicko about the fact that he never wanted to take them off. That was beginning to be so comical. My son really liked his new shoes and was so impressed each time someone complimented them. And the interesting thing about the shoes was that they were a bright color. I would have never thought that he would have worn that color, but he was very happy with them. Go figure! But overall, I was so happy to hear that my son was in a very good mood after the trip home.

On December 2, I received a call from LaRicko's medical doctor informing me that the staff had a meeting earlier that day, and it had been decided in the meeting that LaRicko could go home on December 5. I was so happy to hear that. They also included that he will need to continue therapy for several weeks once he got back to St. Louis. They didn't want him to stay in Mount Vernon until he got despondent, so they allowed us to pick LaRicko up on Friday, the fifth, and the staff selected a rehabilitation facility for my son to attend when he got home. My vision had come to pass. The Lord showed me a vision back in August that my son will be home in five months from the month that he became ill. So I thanked God for blessing us with our miracle. I began to call several family members to share the good news with them. Everyone was so happy for me because it also meant that we didn't have to travel four hours down the road every weekend anymore. The Lord worked it out for us because the winter weather was beginning to set in.

The next couple of days were very exciting for LaRicko. Each time I called to speak with him, he would ask me, "What time are you all going to pick me up?" I must have answered that same question for more than ten times in such a short time. My son was so looking forward to coming home. But LaRicko also was concerned that the doctors were going to change their minds and keep him in the rehabilitation longer, being that a change of the date had happened before. So I tried to assure LaRicko that they were not going to do that anymore. I shared with him that the staff felt that it was okay for him to go home as long as he would get the outpatient therapy sessions set up. LaRicko really didn't like the idea that he had to go to therapy once he made it home, but I shared with him that not only would the therapy help him more during his recovery, it would also allow him to be able to come home on the fifth of December. When I explained it in that way to him, he appeared to accept it better.

On the fifth of December, I could hardly wait to get to Mount Vernon to pick up my son, and I knew he was anxious for us to get there as well. It was so cold that morning and there was ice on the ground, so I really wanted to be careful with my son. Once we made it to the facility, the staff was all gathered around the front desk with sad but, at the same time, happy faces for LaRicko. They did not want to see him leave because he was such a wonderful young man. I asked, "Is he all packed up and ready to go?" The staff began to chuckle and said, "Are you serious? He began packing yesterday, and LaRicko got up early that morning to complete his packing." He wanted to be ready to go as soon as we got there.

As I began to walk down the hall to LaRicko's room, I noticed boxes stacked right at the doorway. I looked over the boxes and saw him sitting in a chair, just waiting for us to get there. I thought it was cute as well as funny! I said, "You boxed yourself in!" He looked up at me, and the only thing LaRicko wanted to know was if we needed him to help us take the boxes to the car. I quickly said no because I didn't want him to go outside in the icy cold weather until it was time for him to leave to head home. Chester (his dad) walked up and looked over the boxes at LaRicko as well, and he asked, "Man, how you are going to get out with all the boxes at the door?"

LaRicko said, "Once you all take the boxes to the car, then I will be right behind you." LaRicko appeared to have a concerned look on his face, as if he thought the doctors were going to change their minds and make him stay longer; he continued to worry about things that weren't even going on. But I kept trying to convince that things were not going to happen like that. After sitting there talking with him for a few minutes while they were getting his release papers ready as well as LaRicko's prescriptions, the counselor that always communicated with me regarding LaRicko's progress walked up to the door and began to talk to LaRicko. She began to tease with LaRicko, and she asked, "Are you sure you are ready to go home?" She was not aware that he was really worried that she was going to make him stay. So that was a touchy question to LaRicko. (How funny.)

The counselor asked me to come with her so that she could share with me all the things that we needed to pursue regarding LaRicko's progress. The counselor shared with me the things that we would all have to focus on, such as his medications and that LaRicko was still pretty weak, for us to make sure that we would watch him carefully going up and down the stairs and while he would get in and out of the tub. I thought it was so nice how the whole staff had so many nice things to say regarding LaRicko that she shared with me. After all the instructions were given to me, LaRicko's dad had finished taking all of LaRicko's things to the car. LaRicko's dad said that he didn't think all the things were going to fit in the car, being that LaRicko had so much stuff. But fortunately, his dad got everything in the car. As we walked back to LaRicko's room to get him so that we could leave, all the staff was standing at the front desk, waiting for him to come down the hall. LaRicko was so relieved that he was actually walking toward the door with me and his father and that no one was saying that he had to stay longer. One guy who had been LaRicko's therapist began to tease LaRicko about leaving those bright-colored shoes with him, and LaRicko chuckled as usual, and everyone began to hug LaRicko while I was snapping pictures of the whole staff. That was a happy and sad day for me as well. The place that I had been commuting back and forth to for the past three and a half months has finally come to an end. I was so happy because it had turned out to be a blessed occasion, and I was sad because I will miss all the wonderful people that supported us through our crisis.

As we were saying our good-byes, the head nurse that worked in the intensive care unit where my son was brought in at the beginning of his condition walked up to me and said, "Thank you for not making a big issue out of the fact that one of our nurses hit your son and was very mean to him. That was not something that we allow at the facility."

I shared with her that the facility had proven to me that there was zero tolerance of being mean to the patients. "As soon as I brought those issues to your attention, you assured that you were going to take care of

*them right away, and you did just that. I would recommend the facility
to anyone," I said to the nurse. I thanked the nurse as I hugged her for
making us feel very comfortable in that area. I shared with the staff that
I was really going to miss all of them. LaRicko even told the staff that he
would look forward to coming back to visit with them in the future.*

*As we began to walk to the elevator to leave the facility, there
were several of the patients that were still there in wheelchairs or
crutches and dealing with several other issues that began to say
good-bye to LaRicko. I remember LaRicko looking so proud and
saying to them, "You will be going home soon." One of the nurses
got on the elevator with us, and other people on the elevator just
made us feel so special. Believe it or not, I almost didn't want to
leave because the people were so wonderful there. But our time there
had expired; it was time for us to move to the next level that God
had prepared for us. I began to thank God for allowing us another
chance with LaRicko.*

*As we began to walk to the car, I made sure that my son was covered
up very well because it was very cold outside. After we got to the car,
I sat in the backseat as LaRicko and Chester sat in the front seats,
preparing for the long drive home. They just didn't know how much joy
I had in my heart from the miracle that the Lord had granted us. That
long test had provided us a wonderful and blessed testimony, which
I was looking forward to sharing with everyone who would listen to
me.*

*After traveling so far on the road, Chester pulled over to a fast-food
restaurant so that LaRicko could stretch his legs as well as go to the
bathroom. I just kind of stood back and watched as LaRicko and his dad*

walked up to the counter to place an order of what LaRicko wanted from the menu. I just thanked God for what may have appeared to be a small thing, such as LaRicko ordering food from the menu, but it was a huge thing for me to be thankful for because five months prior to that date, I was told that my son would never make it to that stage in his life and that he was going to remain in a vegetated state until I had to unplug him. As LaRicko said, God had showed up and was showing out on him. After LaRicko and his dad got their food and went to the bathroom, we headed back to the car (I walked behind LaRicko, making sure that he did not step on any ice or slid, continuing to pray) to continue our journey for home.

Even though it was a very cold day on the fifth of December, we couldn't resist stopping by the hospital where LaRicko had spent fifty-four days of his illness to allow LaRicko to go in and share with their staff his recovery. Of course, I asked my son how he felt regarding the idea. He was anxious to see where he had spent fifty-four days of which he was in a coma, and LaRicko didn't recall any of that.

After four hours of traveling back to St. Louis, we turned off the highway and proceeded to the hospital. As we drove up the lot of the hospital, I watched LaRicko as he was looking around as he if was trying to find something about the area that may have looked familiar to him. When we parked and got out of the car, I began to bundle LaRicko up again because of the cold weather as we walked into the hospital.

We stopped at the gift shop on the first floor, where I pointed out to LaRicko that it was where his uncle (Baba) Horace got the **Fear Not** bracelet that LaRicko was wearing at the time and shared the significance of the prayers that was behind the bracelet. Then we proceeded down *the hall to the second floor, which was the pulmonary floor. That was the floor where a very considerate doctor accepted my son as a patient when all the others turned their back on us.*

As we walked around the corner, I saw the receptionist that was there when we left the hospital to head for Mount Vernon, and she looked at us with a confused facial expression, as if wondering what were we there for. I spoke to her, saying, "This is my son that was in this room" (I pointed to the room across from her desk). I told her that I wanted their staff to see LaRicko after he had recovered. The receptionist's mouth flew open, and she said, "Oh my god." She didn't even recognize LaRicko. She said LaRicko didn't even look like the same young man who left the hospital three and a half months ago. It was another wonderful moment for us. LaRicko smiled as all the other nurses came up to him and began to hug him with excitement in their voices. I will never forget the one nurse named Sharon who had told me that she was sorry to inform me that my son would have never known his unborn child and that his fiancée could just forget about them ever getting married because LaRicko would never be anything but a vegetable. But she also said to me, "Diane, a mother's prayers can go a long way." And that was what I held on to, my faith and prayers.

While we were standing there communicating with the rest of the staff, I asked about Sharon. One of the other nurses said to me, "Oh, Sharon's down the hall; I will go and get her." She informed me that the particular nurse had been having a bad day that day and that Sharon was pretty down in the dumps, and she knew that it would make Sharon's day to see my son. After the nurse went down the hall to get Sharon, a few minutes later, I looked up and saw Sharon running down the hall toward us extremely fast. I remembered thinking to myself, I hope she slows down, because LaRicko was still very, very weak, and I didn't want him to lose his balance and fall if she ran into him. But Sharon didn't stop until she got to LaRicko and wrapped her arms around his neck and just held on to him with tears in her eyes. I placed my hands in LaRicko's back to make sure that he didn't lose his balance and fall as Sharon continued to hold on to him. When she finally let go of LaRicko, she looked at me as she began to hug me and said, "See, Diane, I told you that a mother's prayers will go a long way." I looked her in her eyes and said, "You know, you are right."

After spending quite a bit of time with the staff on the second floor, Chester, LaRicko, and I proceeded to the intensive care unit where LaRicko had spent over a couple of weeks with some very inconsiderate people. But I wanted to let them see my son and how far he had come also. I remembered two of the nurses that were really supportive, Angle and Ben. And I prayed as we headed to the ICU that they would be there so that they could see LaRicko. After I pressed the button that allowed us to enter into the intensive care unit, I actually saw Angle walking out of one of the patient's rooms, and when I called her name, she remembered me by name; that let you to know that our stay was too long there at the hospital. Angle hugged me as she asked, "How did things get with your son?" And I said they went great as I stepped aside and pointed to LaRicko, who was standing a few steps behind me, and at that time, I was glad that I had my hands still around Angle's back because when she looked at LaRicko, she became so weak in her legs that she was going down to the floor. She grabbed her head as she said, "Oh my god, I can't believe this." She walked over and began to hug LaRicko. She turned red as she stood there looking at LaRicko. I asked her if Ben was there, and she said yes as she went back and got him. When Ben walked up, he had to *stare at LaRicko for a moment as he hugged us and said, "These are the kind of visits we love getting." He included that once people leave the hospital, that people didn't usually come back to share with the staff the outcome of their situation. And I told Ben that I was just the opposite; I could hardly wait to come back to share my miracle with the staff (with a proud look on my face as I looked at my son). While visiting with several members of the staff, I even saw the nurse who looked at me as she was caring for my son at the very beginning of LaRicko's illness and said, "Be realistic. Your son is not going to make it out of here alive." That particular nurse stood across the way and just stared over at us. She would not walk over and acknowledge us at all. But that was okay with me, I'm sure she realized at that point that she was not our God.*

As we left the intensive care unit, I felt sad for the people in the overly crowded waiting area. I began to pray within my spirit that those people knew the Lord and that the people would pray and trust God and not depend on man's decision.

Coincidently, as I was walking toward the elevator, I ran into the inconsiderate caseworker who called me at my job and told me to come to the hospital at the beginning of my son's coma condition and gather my son's things and take him home. She was upset with me because she felt that I should just unplug LaRicko or place him in a nursing home where she said he would expire real soon. So when I saw the caseworker, I walked up to her and reminded her of who I was. Wow! She did remember us. When I pointed to LaRicko to let her know that he was blessed and still alive and doing well, I will always remember how that caseworker looked at me very arrogantly and said, "Told you that he would be okay once you take him to Mount Vernon." I looked at her with a confused expression because she knew that wasn't at all the truth. But in my heart, all that was okay because I knew that God had a reason for every avenue that we had to travel.

So after the visit to the hospital, it was time to get LaRicko home because I knew that he was tired after the long ride. As we pulled up in front of his fiancée's house, she was very excited to see him, and he was so happy to see her. I left him to visit her and her family for a while. When I got home, my phone was flooded with messages to find out if we made it back home okay. I felt so loved by so many friends and family members. I just wished that there was a way that I could have shown them all how much I appreciated every last one of them.

Chapter 10

Back to Living Again

The very next day, I got up and prepared breakfast for LaRicko, his fiancée, and friends of mine. I was so excited that my son was actually sitting at my dinner table after being away for so long. That morning was such a fulfilled morning, sitting and listening to LaRicko talk about all the things that he remembered in the past. As we all sat around enjoying each other, the phone began to ring with different family members and friends calling to talk to LaRicko. He was the center of attention, and I could tell that he was appreciating every minute of it.

As the day went on, I called my neighbors over to see LaRicko. They all were so surprised when they walked through my front door and saw LaRicko sitting in the living room.

That was a breathtaking moment for most of them when they walked in. Our neighbors began to share with LaRicko how much they had been praying for him. My next-door neighbor told LaRicko that he had begun asking everyone to pray for me, his mother, because she already felt that LaRicko was not going to make it through that illness alive. My neighbor said that she knew that it would be rough on me once LaRicko had passed away, so she wanted everyone to pray for my strength. But my neighbor included that she was so happy that her thought was wrong. She commended me on my strong faith.

On Sunday, LaRicko was determined to attend church, and I really didn't want him to go out in the cold weather, and at the same time, I was so concerned about him being so weak, but he wanted to bundle up and go anyway. He really was excited about the thought of seeing our pastor as well as hearing our pastor preach his sermon. So that morning, we got to church, and so many people who had been praying with us were so happy to see LaRicko. I even noticed some of the people standing back looking at us as if they saw a ghost and never came up to us to say a word. After church service was over, I walked with LaRicko as he began to walk over and hug our pastor. I think that it just meant so much to LaRicko to hug the pastor because my son really looked up to our pastor.

The first few weeks home, LaRicko had begun his outpatient rehabilitation classes. He really was uncomfortable with the fact of having to go to therapy at another facility, but I reminded him that if he didn't want to attend the outpatient facility, then he would have to go back to Mount Vernon. And as time went on, LaRicko seemed to have come to terms to realize that it was something he had to do. He would get a bit agitated with several things that he had to do in the therapy classes, but I felt as the time went on, he would eventually adjust.

As the next week or so went on, we were closing in on the Christmas holiday. My mother called and said to me that she was going to plan to come up to St. Louis to spend Christmas with LaRicko and me. Mom told me that I had traveled enough miles that year and that she was going to come to St. Louis, which I thought, was really thoughtful of her to say that. My dad wanted to come up here as well but could not get anyone to work in his place at that time. But my dad said that he was going to send his love and blessings, and that was very special for me.

LaRicko and I were so looking forward to the Christmas holiday so that we could put up the Christmas tree together. But before I brought the tree from the basement for us to put it up, I walked with LaRicko to the living room where we shared our last conversation prior to his illness. We had discussed what color of curtains I should choose to place on my four windows in there. After I went out and purchased the curtains and came back to the house that was when LaRicko had suffered a coma. I remembered one of the days I was sitting at home prior to going to the hospital to see LaRicko, I began to change the curtains as I was praying. And a calm voice spoke to me and said, "Change only three of the curtains and leave one for LaRicko to change when he gets home." So I changed three of the curtains in my living room, not caring at that point what it looked like. I was just going to be obedient to the calm voice and be faithful and trust God. As I stood there with LaRicko, sharing that story with him, I pointed to the window where he had to change the curtain. I handed him the curtain that I held on to so faithfully for five months, and I said, "I saved this curtain for you to hang." LaRicko smiled as he struggled to put the curtain on the rod, and of course, I began to take pictures of him with tears of joy in my eyes. Well, after so many months, I finally had all matching curtains in my living room. How funny!

Later that evening, after Chester came over to visit with LaRicko, I asked Chester if he would go down to the basement to bring up the Christmas tree so that LaRicko and I could begin putting it up so that we could decorate it. Chester went down and brought the Christmas tree up for us. I asked LaRicko if he felt like working on the Christmas tree, and he appeared to be okay with the idea. I was really concerned about making my son feel that he was back to his normal self.

As LaRicko and I began to put up the Christmas tree, I was pointing out to him the little ornaments that he made in school when he was in the first grade. I began to share with him how special things such as those were. I had always placed those ornaments on the Christmas tree year after year ever since LaRicko made them in school. He was so proud of the idea as well because he had forgotten that I still had them. I took pictures also as he began to work on putting up the tree and placing ornaments on it. And at the same time, I was praising and thanking God for sparing his life and allowing us to be able to do those things again together.

I will praise thee, O Lord, with my whole heart; I will shew forth all thy marvelous works. (Psalm 9:1)

As the days went on prior to Christmas, while LaRicko and I were sitting around talking, he asked, "Mom, do you think I will ever be able to run again?"

"Of course," I said to him.

What I thought was so interesting was that I had never thought about the fact that my son could not run, forgetting that he really had to start all over again as a newborn baby would have. So I got up and began to move the furniture in the living room and in the dining room area all to one side of the house. I stood to the side as I said to LaRicko, "Try and run from the hallway to the front door." I watched him closely as a mother would a one-year-old, praying that he wouldn't trip and fall. But he was so determined to do it. It really was a struggle for my son to run because he could barely lift his feet up. I watched him for as long as he wanted to struggle to run back and forth in the house. I told LaRicko that as long as he would keep up the good work in trying to run, before he knew it, he would be running as fast as he used to before all that happened to him. He began to smile as he continued to run from the door back to the hallway, and I stood off to the side and watched him, but close enough to catch him if he would accidentally stumble and fall. We continued to do that as often as LaRicko wanted to.

It had gotten closer to Christmas, and LaRicko's aunt Lela wanted to go Christmas shopping. So LaRicko and I went along with her. I was kind of surprised at that point that LaRicko wanted to go to the stores in such blistering cold weather, but he was raring to go. When we got to the shopping mall, we walked around to several stores, and he appeared to enjoy the holiday spirit that was going on around us. As we were walking down one end of the mall, I began to notice several young men gathering around us, making some threatening comments behind LaRicko and I, and I was wondering to myself what was going on. LaRicko said to me, "Mom, those guys are talking to me." I asked him why, and LaRicko replied, "Because of the color of the jacket I'm wearing!" They actually wanted to jump on my son for that stupid reason. I thought to myself, Some of our people are really sick. I really wanted to turn and say something to them because I was not going to allow anyone to hurt my baby. We had come too far for something such as that, but I knew that we were outnumbered, so I began to pray because at that point, that was all I could do, and you know I know what prayers can do. Because I wasn't going to allow those guys to harm my son for one minute, I would have allowed them to hurt me first. After a few minutes of praying, those guys eventually walked to the other side of the mall and went on about their business. The enemy was still busy! We walked into one of the stores at the mall where LaRicko saw a beautiful big picture with a rose on it, and it said Mother, Your Heart is Like a Rose. LaRicko picked up the picture and read it and went straight the counter to pay for it. He said that he thought that it was the perfect Christmas gift for me. I thought that was sweet of him to buy it for me, but he just didn't know I had all the Christmas presents I needed at that point. I had my wonderful son with me, and I didn't care about any other material things for Christmas. But once we got back to the house, I pointed out to him where I was going to hang the picture to get his thoughts, which was on the wall right in front of my bed so that it would be the first thing I see when I wake up in the morning and the last thing I look at when I lay down in the bed at night, and he thought that was a great idea. And that's exactly where we hung it. I love the beautiful picture.

At Christmastime, my mother and my nephews Gene and Kiwon came up and spent time with us, which was really, really a blessed Christmas. Mom and Dad had bought LaRicko and me so many nice gifts. As the day went on, so many family members came over to visit with us. Later that day, we went over to visit with some family members and took LaRicko with us. So many of our family members were speechless because they could not believe who they were seeing (LaRicko). It was so overwhelming for some of my cousins. They did not expect LaRicko to make it out of his illness alive. That is why I continue to thank God for showing up and showing out for us. We have an awesome testimony! As time went on, we continued to take things one day at a time with LaRicko's recovery. We went through a wonderful and blessed New Year, and after that, I began to look forward to the birth of my first grandbaby. My grandbaby was expected to be arriving on January 16, and with all the things that had been going on in our lives the past few months, I really hadn't had time to plan or even think about a baby shower. But as I began to talk to different people around me and at my job, everyone thought the week after New Year would be a perfect time than ever to have a baby shower.

Being that it was a bit late to think about sending out baby shower invitations, I began to get on the phone and call several family members and friends. It was so blessed because everyone that I called said that they would be there. So I managed to get a baby shower all together in one week.

When the day came for the baby shower, I will never forget it. It was so cold, raining, and sleeting. I really didn't think too many people would show up because of the weather. But to my surprise, everyone showed up that was invited and more. We began to play games as they dressed LaRicko and his fiancée up in funny-looking attire. That was so nice to see them sitting there together when the doctor said it would never happen. LaRicko and his fiancée began to open the gifts after we were done playing games and eating. Everyone was awesome to them because they received all kinds of gifts for the baby. They had gotten so many gifts; we could not get them all in the car that night as his fiancée prepared to go home in the freezing rain. I dropped them off, and when I finally got back home, I made sure that I took out the time to pray and thank God for continuing to show up and show out in our lives.

One of my cousins who I was very, very close to, and our kids grew up together. It was the cousin who took me to Red Lobsters earlier in my story who called me the very next day, which was Sunday. She shared with me how, during the time of LaRicko illness, she had seen patients in the condition that LaRicko was in during her years of experience in nursing. And she shared with me that she didn't want to tell me at the time of my son's illness, but she just knew LaRicko was not going to make it. My cousin said that she had seen people in LaRicko's condition, and they had never made it out alive. But she told me after she came over to the baby shower that evening at my house, and as she sat down and talked with him in the kitchen as they ate ice cream, my cousin said that she could not believe the conversation that they shared. My cousin said to me when she got up Sunday morning, it was raining very hard and it was very cold, but she was determined to go to church because after seeing what God had done for my son, she could hardly wait to go and join church. She included that no matter what type of weather it was that morning, she was not going to allow it to keep her from church. I had tears of joy in my eyes, and I said, "Praise the Lord." I knew that the entire situation that LaRicko and I *had gone through was not about us; it was all about the Lord. To God be the glory.*

After a long tiring day at work, I was anxious to get home and to relax for the evening. As soon as I walked into the door, I received a call from my son's fiancée to let him know that her water had broke, and she and her mom were on their way to the hospital, and they wanted us to meet them there. Well, needless to say, LaRicko and his dad, Chester, were out visiting with several other friends and family members and that neither one of them had a cell phone. That was my first grandbaby, and I was eager to get to the hospital before she arrived, but I couldn't leave home until LaRicko and his dad got back to the house. So as I paced the floor, I ran back and forth to the door, looking out for them to drive up. I was saying to myself, I can't believe this is happening. I was about to leave the house without them because I didn't want to miss the delivery of my grandbaby when LaRicko and his dad finally drove up. I walked out the door and told them that we needed to head to the hospital. I told LaRicko that his baby was on the way. I couldn't tell from his facial expression whether he was ecstatic or not. It appeared that he was in shock. I was praying that the excitement was not too much for LaRicko too soon, being that he was still going through his recovery stage.

Once we got to the hospital, his fiancée was still being prepped to prepare for the delivery. I thanked God that we made it to the hospital before she had LaRicko's first child. I was thinking about how LaRicko probably would have felt if he had missed the delivery of their daughter. Believe it or not, if we had shown up six or seven hours later, we still would have been on time. After rushing to the hospital around 5:30 p.m. in the evening, my grandbaby was not born until 1:30 a.m. in the morning. It was such a blessing because as I sat out in the waiting area waiting on the baby to be delivered and my son was in the delivery room with his fiancée, I began to ponder about what the doctors had said a few months ago regarding LaRicko being brain-dead. I was praying and thanking God for ordering my steps to do the right thing, which was to hold and trust God. To God be the glory!

As I began to hear the loud cry from my grandbaby, my eyes began to fill up with tears. The date was January 14, two days before the scheduled time for my grandbaby to arrive. It showed us that things happen at God's timing and not before. The very next day was LaRicko's birthday, and he had prayed that his daughter wouldn't be born on his birthday because he said he wanted his daughter to have her own little day, and she did. She was born the day before LaRicko's birthday. I walked into the room where my grandbaby was born; I noticed that LaRicko had such a proud look on his face. I was so happy that he was there supporting his fiancée through the whole thing. As the evening went on, LaRicko began to get a bit upset because everyone was saying how much his daughter looked just like his fiancée. LaRicko went into the men's bathroom and he stayed in there for so long that I began to worry about him because he was still very weak and he was on tons of medication. So I began to knock on the bathroom door, and when LaRicko eventually walked to the door, I asked him what the problem was. As he stood there with tears in his eyes, he said to me, "Mom, the one thing that I feel I have in my life is my daughter, and everyone is trying to take her by saying she looks just like my fiancée." I knew that LaRicko was still being very, very sensitive. At that point, I hugged him and told him that, "Your daughter has just arrived, just give her some time, she will probably look just like you in the future." And I continued with, "No one can ever take your daughter from you." I knew that we still had challenges to work out with LaRicko, and I was okay with that.

I was just happy to have him here with us at such a joyous time. After his fiancée was placed in her room after the delivery, I was so tired after sitting for so long that I went home to get some rest. I was finally a proud grandmother!

After I got up the next day, we went to the hospital to visit with my grandbaby. My granddaughter was a little doll. After a while, I left LaRicko and his fiancée at the hospital to enjoy their newborn as I went to pick up a birthday cake for the very next day, which was January 15, to take to the hospital and celebrate LaRicko's twenty-seventh birthday. It was one great big celebration. Spending time at a hospital ended up being a positive time for a change!

As the days went on, LaRicko was being a happy and supportive dad and fiancé. I was very proud of him doing as well as he was so soon. I felt that being that he was a father; it allowed him to try even harder to get stronger faster.

In February around Valentine's Day, LaRicko and his fiancée and I decided to go down to visit our family in Arkansas. I was so proud of my grandbaby, who I wanted to show off to everyone that I could. And I knew that LaRicko wanted to show his daughter off as well, being that she was his first child.

After visiting with the family for a few days, it finally came up to the time that we needed to head back to St. Louis. As we traveled down the highway headed back home, LaRicko wanted to stop in West Memphis to get something from Walmart. I sat in the car with my grandbaby while LaRicko and his fiancée went inside to do some shopping. After LaRicko and his fiancée returned to the car, I began to drive off the parking lot.

On the way to the highway, LaRicko said to me from the backseat of the car, "Mom, we are going to get married on the twenty-fourth of April." I really didn't understand him the first time that he said it, so I asked, "What did you say, baby?" And he repeated, "Me and my fiancée are going to get married on the twenty-fourth of April." As I continued to drive, I began to think to myself, was the detour to Walmart a setup or what? Did they go into the store so that they could come up with a game plan of how they were going to share the news with me? The only thing that I could say behind that shocking statement was okay. I began to get a bit numb, but it was a happy numb feeling. I was just completely caught off guard with such a short time frame to prepare for a wedding.

As we continued to travel down the road headed home, his fiancée and I began to discuss some wedding plans. After a few minutes of discussing several things regarding the wedding plans, I actually began to get a little excited. I was actually beginning to feel that things were finally falling into place for us once again.

After we returned home, I got on the phone right away and began to call several friends and family members to share with them that we had a short time to plan a wedding. Everyone that I spoke with was in just as much shock as I was, but was willing to do whatever was needed to help. As the time went on, I wrote up a list of names of the people that I was going to contact to get their addresses in order to mail them an invitation, and as I was doing that, it came to my mind to contact several of the people that were supportive to us while he was at the hospital as well as the people at the rehabilitation center.

One of the laboratory technicians had given me her phone number prior to us leaving the hospital and asked if I would keep in touch with her to share with her how LaRicko was doing. So I thought that it would be a great time to touch bases with her to share how well he was doing as well as invite several nurses of the staff to LaRicko's wedding. When I called her and she answered the phone, she was so jubilant to hear from me. I shared with her how LaRicko was doing as well as him getting married in the next couple months. She was elated! I told her that I would be thrilled if she would come to the wedding. And she said that she would be honored. So as we went on with our conversation, I began to ask her about several other nurses by name because I had them all written down in my journal that I kept each day when we were at the hospital.

Each person that I asked about, she would tell me that they were doing fine, and she would share with me what shift that the person was working so that I would know the best time to take the wedding invitation to them. As I went on with my questions, I couldn't help but ask about the one nurse that would so quietly walk into my son's room in the middle of the night, around the twenty-ninth of August. That particular nurse had always stuck out in my mind for some reason because I was a bit upset with her the night that she stood over the head of my son's bed and told me to tell my son that he was in the hospital and share with LaRicko why he was in the hospital and continue to pray for my son. And I remember on that Friday night in August, as that nurse was saying these things, LaRicko began to cry. I did not like the fact that she had been upsetting my son by saying those things. I was so busy trying to protect him from being disturbed by several things that I missed the fact at the time that LaRicko was showing signs of emotions, and a brain-dead person wouldn't have been able to focus on anything such as that. When I asked the technician about that particular nurse, she said to me, "We don't have anyone here by that name."

I asked, *"Are you sure?"* The technician answered me, saying, *"No, we've never had anyone here by that name."* So I began to look in my journal, which I knew that I had documented every day, very carefully each person's name that had worked with my son to assure myself that I was asking for the correct name. And I'll never forget the technician saying in such a nice but convincing voice, *"No, we've never had a nurse by that name."*

So I began to go a step further to think, Maybe I wrote down the wrong name, which I knew I kept my journal very accurately. I began to describe the nurse to her. I said that the nurse that I was speaking of had an afro, and she was kind of light brown in complexion. The tech said, *"No. No one such as that description has worked for our hospital, on our shift."* The technician wanted to convince me even further by saying that she had been employed at the hospital for over ten years, and she had never met anyone of that stature.

As I began to thank her for all the information that she had shared with me, I said to her that I will be looking forward to seeing her at LaRicko's wedding.

Of course, when I hung up the phone from speaking with the lab technician, I couldn't help but sit there and ponder over what the technician had said to me regarding the nurse that had never worked there. I began to pray, and tears came to my eyes as I thought about that entire evening that the nurse was in my son's room. So I sat there and began to cry because there's time, as I had said earlier in the book that God shows up and we don't recognize him. And I began to think about the fact that when LaRicko began to cry that Friday night after the nurse came into the room talking to me regarding my son, it was actually the first time that LaRicko began to show emotions. I began to cry even harder as I thought about the scripture, which said, "When I was hungry you did not feed me." And I think about times when people on the street will ask you for money or food, and we never know, there may be a time when the Lord may show up, and we miss him. The Lord showed up for us! I was so emotional the rest of the day after having the conversation with the technician. As time had gone on, I couldn't even share that testimony with anyone because I would tear up too much.

Well, the time had come for LaRicko and his fiancée to have a wedding rehearsal. His fiancée had planned for the wedding to take place outside, which was at a backyard of a family friend. The yard was huge as well as beautiful. I felt that we were taking a great chance to plan an outside wedding, being that the weather could change at any moment because it was in the month of April, and with April, we have the April showers. I asked his fiancée if she was going to plan a backup facility in case of rainy weather. She said no, she was just going to plan to have it in the beautiful backyard.

It was the weekend for LaRicko and his fiancée's wedding, and we were being bombarded with so many blessed family and friends. So I was extremely tired after trying to help with the wedding plans as well as entertaining. As the evening went on, LaRicko's brother, Michael, came over to pick him up to take him out for a bachelor party. Even though I knew that his brother, Michael, was going to take care of him, I was still a bit concerned being that LaRicko was yet in a recovering stage from the illness. I sat up most of the night until my son returned home. When LaRicko got home and began to prepare himself for bed, I finally took the opportunity to relax and lay my head down on my pillow. *Needless to say, I didn't get any sleep that night.*

The day had come for LaRicko and his fiancée to become husband and wife. So many of our family members and friends had traveled from a far distance to be there in St. Louis with us on LaRicko's special occasion, which was such a blessing. As I lay there trying to relax for at least an hour, I couldn't help but listen to the hard raindrops hitting the windows. I knew that his fiancée had planned an outdoor wedding, but needless to say, I did not get discouraged at all. I began to pray and thank God for whatever he had planned for us that day; just lead us to it. Of course, the enemy tried to dampen my spirit a couple of times because I knew that his fiancée was looking forward to having her wedding in the beautiful backyard that she had picked out. But I had begun to think about all the blessings that had happened on a hard rainy day. One of the things that came to my mind was back when my son was in a coma and I was sitting in his hospital room looking out of the window at the hard raindrops falling, I began to pray; and as I looked around at LaRicko lying there in his bed, he began to try and sit up, and I walked over to assist him in sitting up. So with that in mind, I did not get disappointed about the rain at all because I knew that wonderful and blessed things could happen on a rainy day. So as everyone began to prepare themselves for the special day, we were beginning to receive calls from different people from the guest list to find out where we were going to relocate the wedding, being that it was raining. Things actually fell into place for us as I knew they would. As the afternoon came, the guests began to show up for such a wonderful occasion. It was such an emotional time for several people because LaRicko was such a miracle. On that day, things were taking place, which the doctors had said would never happen. I was such a proud and blessed mother. When LaRicko *and Chester showed up, I began to hug my son and share with him how happy and proud I was of him. When I looked LaRicko in his eyes, he looked as if he had been crying. I asked LaRicko if he was okay, and he said he was fine. I began to wonder if my son was beginning to have cold feet and wanted to change his mind about getting married. So as LaRicko walked into the room where his groomsmen were waiting, I pulled his dad to the side and asked him if LaRicko had been crying. His dad said yes. At that moment, my heart dropped because I didn't want him to do something that he didn't want to do. So I asked Chester, "What seems to have been the problem?" And I thought it was kind of funny that Chester looked at me and said, "Don't you think that he is happy as well? This is his wedding day, and LaRicko was saying to me on the way here that he is such a blessed person to be able to do this when the doctor said it would never happen." I had to remind myself that God had brought us too far for me to continue to be concerning myself with the negative thoughts. The enemy just kept trying to creep into my spirit.*

The wedding had begun, and I was taken down the aisle first and sat right down in the front row. I was so excited to see how many people showed up for us on such a rainy day. Wow! There I was with my new grandbaby, and I was about to become a mother-in-law in a matter of minutes. All those things were such a nice thought to me.

I sat there and watched as all the bridesmaids and the groomsmen began to come down the aisle. It was such a beautiful wedding even though we had to reroute everything because of the rain at the last minute. God really was working things out for us, even with the rain, because the Lord is the rainmaker. Shortly afterward, everyone else had come down the aisle, and there came the beautiful bride. I watched my son as he stood there looking at his bride as she walked toward him. I could see happiness in their eyes as they looked at each other. Lots of the friends and family members that were in the crowd were in tears. It was such a special moment for all of us. It was an event that we were told that was never going to happen. But it did on April 24. Praise the Lord!

After the minister completed all the vows, she pronounced them husband and wife. I'll never forget how my daughter-in-law and LaRicko turned toward each other and saluted each other with a huge kiss. I was so happy for both of them. And in my heart, I felt that they deserved all the happiness that was coming their way after everything that they had gone through. At that point, we could see that God delays things in our lives for reasons, and we should keep in mind that delay does not mean denied.

After the wedding, we continued to the reception part of the occasion. I mingled with the crowd, thanking everyone for their prayers and blessings that they had granted us. As I stood back and watched LaRicko, I could see such a proud look on his face, and I was actually excited to see that. LaRicko's brother, Michael, made such a short and sweet toast to his brother. He said to LaRicko, "Your bride was your first, your last, and your everything," and the crowd began to laugh as Michael and the rest of the wedding party toasted and took a sip from their glasses.

As the wedding celebration began to come to an end and people were beginning to leave, LaRicko's dad, Chester, drove LaRicko and his bride to their honeymoon suite for the evening. And I left the reception and headed for home riding in the rain and enjoying my parents, brothers, and my aunt and uncle around me. I was saying silent prayers to the Lord, thanking him for showing people that he is in control of our lives and that he is in the miracle-working business. Not only am I a mother-in-law, I am also a proud grandmother. Praise the Lord.

I will praise thee, O Lord, with my whole heart; I will shew forth all thy marvelous works. (Psalm 9)

The next day, our families prepared themselves for the long journey back to Memphis, Arkansas, Michigan, Mariana, Chicago, and several other places. I prayed and thanked God for all of them to have a safe and blessed trip back to their destinations.

As the months went on, LaRicko, his wife, and my grandbaby continued to live happily ever after. One year later from the date that LaRicko came up to St. Louis for the weekend and went into a coma, his dad, Chester, and I moved them back to Memphis, Tennessee, where LaRicko is residing and is very happy. Everything happened at God's timing, not ours!

Epilogue

Just know that this book was not at all written to try and make anyone (hospitals or doctors) look bad at any angle or to appear that the staff was not doing their jobs properly. As I look back on my situation, I feel that my situation was a spiritual walk with the Lord, and it was not at all an easy walk. This story is to allow everyone to know that just because a condition or a situation does not feel good to us or look good does not mean that you are being attacked by the enemy. For a long time, I felt that my son's condition was a punishment to me from the Lord for something that I may have done in my life. But a lot of praying and encouragement from others helped me to understand that our God is not a petty God; he does not react toward us like everyday people. God has his way of molding us into what our purpose in life is. And there will be times that we will go through our storms in life and be brought out, but God says you are not ready yet, and before we know it, we are back in the storm again. Keep in mind that God is not finish with us yet.

Since this situation happened to me, I have prayed and asked the Lord to show me my purpose in life. I have struggled with that question for quite some time. I can't help but think of all the people that I've met through this walk. I've thought of the people in the hospital that were going through their crisis at the same time as I was and how I tried to encourage them, even though my son was pronounced to be brain-dead. But I always found myself trying to inspire that next person, no matter how I was feeling inside. So as I continued to pray and fast, I felt that this was the beginning of my purpose in life. I want to encourage and inspire someone with my story. And the Lord spoke to me and said, "Share your story with everyone that you can. Write a book and begin inspiring people in this way." I realize that this is not at all about me or LaRicko, but it is about the Lord.

The roads that we travel in life a lot of times may not feel good to us, but it could be the road that leads you to your purpose in life. I've thought back several times to the areas that I had to go during my son's illness. It is so amazing to me all the things that I had to see in the hospital and the rehabilitation centers. On a normal day, I know that I could not have been able to handle a lot of those things that I had to see, but being that my son was there, I was able to walk with my head up and inspire people along the way, looking to the Lord to guide me and to give me strength all along the way.

In this book, I also shared where God showed up for us, and because things didn't appear to me like I wanted them to, I almost missed that the Lord had showed up for us. On that Friday night, a nurse came into my son's room and told me to talk to my son and tell him what happened to him as well as to let him know that he was in the hospital. The moment my son started to cry, I became disappointed with the nurse, as I shared with you in my story, because I felt that the nurse was upsetting my son. Now I realize that God had showed up, and I was caught up in not wanting to see my son cry that I missed the fact that my son was showing signs of emotion. So as I've said, when I called to invite that particular nurse to my son's wedding, I was told that the nurse had never worked at that hospital, and the technician went as far as to share with me that no one by that name had ever worked there before. When Prophet Michael came into our lives, I was really excited to meet a prophet. I remember in my story where he said to me, "Diane do not fight where God is taking you." And I said to him, "I'll never do that." But the Lord has spoken to me several times to share my story in a book. But I'd find myself doing other things, and I'd place this down for another date. I was always working, putting in long hours and not doing what God said for me to do. And as time went on, through my disobedience, I began to feel like Jonah who ended up in the belly of the fish because of his disobedience.

As time went on and things in my life began to get worse and worse, I sat down and asked the Lord what he has for me to do, and he kept speaking to me, saying, "Share your story in a book." Just know that when God has something for you to do, there is no way that you're going to get out of it. You can fight it, like I did, but you are only hurting yourself and wasting precious time.

Since LaRicko's recovery, I've sat down and talked with him on several different occasions regarding what he'd gone through. Whenever LaRicko wants to talk about what he went through during his coma, I'd always take the time to listen because I have wondered if a comatose patient could hear or if it was just reflexes, as I was told.

And in asking LaRicko questions about this, he began to share all that he could remember, all the way back to right before he went in a coma. LaRicko shared with me what he remembered up to the day that he went to visit the friend in the neighborhood. He said that the friend and three other guys along with himself were sitting around, talking and enjoying catching up on old times, and he shared with them his future plans and how things were finally looking up for him, and they all appeared to be happy for him. Then he said the next thing he knew, he woke up in this friend's basement, and no one was there but him. So LaRicko said when he got up and walked around the corner to our house, that's when he met me at the steps after I'd gone home from church. He'd get pretty disturbed about this when he talks about it because he felt that his so-called friends were trying to harm him, but through this crisis that has happened to him, he has said to me, "Mom, you've always told me that you have to be careful of how you use the word friend." They left him alone in a basement and never once came to me and said anything through LaRicko's entire illness. I didn't have anything to go on. But at the same time, this is where God showed up and showed out. And I'd tell my son that the Lord will fight our battles for us.

LaRicko also included that the things that would come to his mind was what he remembered us saying to him while he was in a coma. He said there were times that when I wasn't at the hospital and the nurses would do or say certain things about him that he didn't like, he'd say to himself, I can't wait 'til my mom gets here so that I can tell her. But once I showed up at the hospital, LaRicko said that he couldn't get the words out. One day LaRicko began to tell me that while he was in his coma, it was as if he was in a courtroom with the Lord, and he was on the witness stand. He said it was as if the Lord weighed the good things that he'd done against the bad things that he'd done, and once it was evaluated, the Lord told him that he was going to give him another chance with life. And LaRicko said afterward, he felt that this was when he began to come out of the comatose state condition one step at a time. LaRicko continues to share different things with me to this day as it come to his mind regarding being in a coma. It is interesting what a comatose patient could be going through. That's why I'd like to encourage loved ones to always talk to your family members if they are in this condition. Pray with them and let them know that they are not alone; you're going to be with them through it all.

*Every avenue you travel in life is not always your purpose; it could be leading you to your purpose. Remember . . . **No pain, no gain!***

There's never a testimony without the test.

Lightning Source UK Ltd.
Milton Keynes UK
UKHW042257011218
333261UK00001B/117/P